SPLINTERED

BROKENNESS IN THE POLITICAL ARENA

I0122746

Are We Sacrificing America for Political Gain?

You be the Judge~

VIVIAN L. CHILDS

SPLINTERED
Copyright © 2014 by Vivian L. Childs

V.L. Childs /UICF LLC
P.O. Box 9334
Warner Robins, GA 31095
splintered@vlchilds.com

.

Author: Vivian L. Childs
Editorial Team: Nakeisha Curry, Judy Dienst,
& Ashante Everett
Cover design: Vivian L. Childs

Printed in the United States of America

ISBN: 978-0-9799896-43

Splintered

TABLE OF CONTENTS   Pages

SPLINTERED

Dedication

This book is dedicated to America and the many *men and women* who sacrifice their lives for the freedom and security of us all. Thank you, daddy, for teaching me to care.

In Memory of:

Senior Chief Isaiah Clark
(retired after 28 years in the US Navy)

SPLINTERED

Preface

This book is a collection of thoughts from individuals involved in some way, in the political process. The thoughts are from college students, educators, a community activist, veterans, clergy, a consultant, a physician, and a former congressional candidate. The common thread, shared by all, is that they believe America is worth their commitment and their sacrifice. The question is, do you? The intent of this book is to serve as a blueprint for the importance of putting America first. Please read this as it is intended.

I am so honored to be able to write an endorsement for Vivian. She and I have worked together for many years for things we both believed in and supported to the ultimate. Her untiring effort and hard work has benefited so many people whose lives she has impacted through the years. Her faith in God, her loyalty, her conservatism, her integrity, and her big heart are only a few of the assets of this amazing woman. I am blessed to be called her friend. I submit this with so much pride and love for you, Vivian.

Gloria Alday, political activist for 20 years
GAGOP Past Vice Chairman,
Former Houston County Commissioner

Disclaimer: *The views and opinions expressed in this book are those of the individual writers. Enjoy~*

Foreword

Helen Clark

I, Aralyn Y. Everett, am the granddaughter of Henry and Vivian Childs and I interviewed my Great Grandmother, Big Mama, for the foreword of this book, *Splintered*. My Big Mama said that Gran-Gran is one of the best daughters any one can have. She said it took her and Chief five years from the birth of their first child to have my Gran-Gran and when she was born, they knew God had sent them an *angel*. She said Gran-Gran came here differently and she is still different today.

Big Mama said, "Vicky is the drum major of her own band; she keeps in step with the Lord, not man. When she is your friend, you have a friend indeed. She does not care about your status in life, your status in politics, or how much money you have in the bank. She treats everybody the same. Our family has been blessed to see Vicky's heart through her caring, day to day living. You, the reader, will be blessed to see Vicky's heart through the stroke of a computer key. To know her is to love her; we do."

"Vicky is kind, sweet, loving, and a helping hand. She loves people, does great things for people, and is always willing to take care of others. I couldn't ask for a better daughter than Vicky or share a better person with others. She readily gives advice, great advice, and is always there to take children under her arm. Vicky (most of her family calls her Vicky, but you know her as Vivian), your mother, Mrs. Helen Clark, will always love you and is proud that you have written a book that will help others bring our country back together again through love for one another."

Your mom, *Helen Clark*

Aralyn Y. Everett

Gran-Gran, I enjoyed interviewing my Big Mama. I think you are the kindest, most sweetest person there is. You are the *light* in the dark, the *flame* to the candle. You are one of the best things that has ever happened to me. I love you so much; words cannot even explain my love for you. I do hope that one day, I will turn out like you. You are perfect to me. You make mistakes, but then fix them and they always change my life.

One day I will follow in your footsteps. It may not be today or tomorrow, but one day. I could not ask for a better grandma (Gran- Gran) than you, Mrs. Vivian Childs. I will always love you from the bottom of my heart.

Aralyn Y. Everett

SPLINTERED

Chapter One

▸What Happened?

A re we engaged in a Civil War, politically? Ask yourself as I have, what happened, and why?   Many are reaping the benefits of strife, diligence, strength, courage, patience, and determination. What happened to an undeniable will and a burning desire to put others before self? What happened to doing, no matter who gets the credit? I mean, what happen-ed? Somewhere, somehow, we lost sight of the prize. The prize being *America*. Somewhere, somehow, we forgot how we achieved and reached the success that many of us are reaping the benefits of today. Truly, it bothers me and to be perfectly honest, it sickens me, how our divisiveness is leading to the demise of this great country. Will someone please tell me what happened?

Achievements, at one time, focused on using the strength of everyone involved. Everyone had a seat at the table. No talent or gift was cheapened by who you were or who you knew. This country, the United States of America, was built because of our diversity. Our greatness is a result of the contributions from different races, genders, cultures, languages, ideas, and yes, political parties. But today, when we should be smarter than ever, we want everyone to be put in a box where everyone is a stereotype, carbon copy, or mirror of someone else.

Some speak of America as a melting pot. By design, we would be this harmonious nation whereby all who enter America would embrace American lifestyles and live as one country, one culture, instead of one country, many cultures. As you can see, that is not America today. The problem with being a melting pot is exactly what it says; once everyone is thrown into the same pot and begins to melt together, everyone in the pot will begin to lose, if not careful, their innovation, their ideas, their creativity, and yes, even their identity.

In years past, we proudly sang "My County 'tis of thee, sweet land of liberty." This is contrary to a shirt I read recently that said, "My country 'tis of me, me, me, me, me, me, me." This is a sad, comical, but oh so true statement of what America has become.

Because of the unity of the past, unlike the *splintering* of today, I stand proudly, a woman who sat in the back of the bus, drank from colored water fountains, lived on (what was to some, but not to me) one of the worse streets in the neighborhood; yet, I have had the privilege to live on an island in the Portugal region where I supped with the *Brigadeiro* and was afforded the opportunity to introduce a former First Lady of the United States of America during a military tour.

> *Why then do children today have no hope for the future?*
> *Where are the trailblazers?*
> *Where are the Harriet Tubman's?*
> *Where are the Frederick Douglass'?*
> *Where are the Abraham Lincoln's?*
> *Where are our ladders to success?*

What happened?

Are we no longer reaching back and bringing others forward when we move forward? If we must mimic, are we mimicking those who went before us, made the sacrifices, opened the doors, and helped shape America's future? If the answer is no, then I must ask you again, what happened?

One thing is for sure: we are eating our own simply because of our differences. Instead of celebrating our differences, we are being ridiculed for them. *No Child Left Behind* left too many behind. Growing up, we catered to our children's strengths and allowed them success in those strengths and masters of a skill. Today, we crucify teachers for poor performance of students; however, many teachers are no longer allowed creativity in teaching. Everyone is doing the same thing and our kids are being taught to be test-takers instead of critical thinkers. We focus too much on learning what is in our comfort zone rather than looking to see what is outside of the box. For example, why can't we teach, just teach, because the subject matter needs to be taught. I don't care why $2 + 2 = 4$. No amount of fingers, manipulatives, or standards come into play when you are in a grocery store and need to count your money. I know people in their eighties who run circles around the younger generation in doing simple math. Why, because they know what they need to know about math to survive outside of the classroom and frankly, that is enough. Sorry, $2 + 2 = 4$, because it does. Period. Save the theory (insanity for some) for those who wish to further their education in a math concentration and allow parents, minus the frustration, the ability to help with homework at home, or do not call it homework.

An example: A young man came to me because he had not passed the math portion of the CRCT; he was scheduled to retake the test on the following Monday. He came to me the Thursday before the test. Yes, I could teach him the method shown in the book, but he had a math block, a fear of failure. So, I had him locate and circle problems in the math book that he was struggling with, so I could begin to assist in his simplified learning of math. This particular young man was convinced that he was not smart in math and would definitely not be able to learn in a few days what he had not learned all year. I explained to the young man and to his mother that I would be able to teach him to get the correct answers, but the method I would teach him was not feasible for use in the classroom. My method of teaching required using fewer steps, creating fewer chances to make mistakes, and my method was precise, quick, to the point, and gave the young man an opportunity for success on future tests. Oh, by the way, the young man passed the math retake, on the CRCT, the following Monday.

Here is another example for restoring math to real-life computation. While standing in line at a popular retail store recently, my daughter was stunned by what she observed during what should have been a simple checkout. A man who did not speak English well, but obviously performed math well, was having difficulty receiving the correct change. Why? The total for the transaction was $15.03. The cashier entered that the customer gave her $20.00. However, he had given the cashier $20.03 and the confusion began; the cashier was lost. She could not understand why he gave her three pennies and because he did, she did not know where to begin. His family tried to explain, as my daughter did, to simply give the customer five dollars to complete the transaction. The cashier stated that she was not authorized to reset the amount paid and that she did not have a calculator to compute the appropriate change due to the customer. Her computer (based on $20.00 given) stated that she owed the gentlemen $4.97. She could not understand why he was giving her three pennies (although everyone else in line knew that he was just trying to get $5.00 back) so, she had to ask her elderly supervisor for assistance. It was so sad because this young cashier had no idea why that made sense. The supervisor, an older woman, came and solved the confusion immediately. What are we doing to math? What happened?

A Moment to Remember!

I remember it well, *"We are a proud people."* Those are the words that were chanted when it seemed that we had no hope in this country that we call America: *Land of the free* and *Home of the brave.* Free for whom, I ask, because it sure was not for me. I sometimes feel hurt and angry when I think about how men and women fought and blazed a trail for the generation that would follow. America, Americans fought a good fight of faith, hope, and many times misery, so that we all, not just some, could enjoy all that America has to offer.

During the sixties and seventies, many fought like proud warriors and sustained many insults and injuries in a quest for freedom. Much was gained in those years. So, what happened? I will tell you what happened. Individuals seemed to get complacent and because some were "making it," too many forgot about those who had not. In that era, individuals were smart enough to know that in order to advance and move forward (sit-ins, boycotts, well thought-out tactics), they required unity.   Everyone in my community, woman, man, or child was a brother or a sister. If one made it, that person would reach back and pull another person up. We lived in an *all about us* society. Today, we live in an *all about me* society.

It is every man for himself and, "Oh, well" with everyone else. Through unity and determination, all kinds of barriers were broken (segregation, colored fountains and bathrooms, as well as sitting on the back of a bus) and here we are (over fifty years later) and at least to me, have not written many more pages in the history books except in entertainment. Why? Because we are *splintered*, not unified.

There once was a time when individuals were taught that a *good* education was what was needed to make something of their lives. Success was looked upon as something earn-ed, instead of something given.

I am reminded of the ant. No one fears standing alone on an ant. But if there is an ant-hill, a totally different scenario, you avoid it like the plague. Why? Strength. When we unify, we are victorious; we are strong; we are innovative.   Re-member... where there is unity, there is victory.

Refresh my memory. What is this nation called?   Is it called the states of America?   No, it is not. It is called the United States of America: United... unity. One nation under God;   not divided, but *United* we stand. So what are we doing? Proud to be an American, but take delight in oppos-ing even the smallest things. What has happened to coming together for the good of all? What has happened to a sense of family, a sense of community, and a sense of party?

In this country, we are willing to destroy a man or woman's life, just to win...to gain the world, but lose your soul. Is it worth it? What are we doing? Where is the unity? When did winning, by destroying ones character and taking delight in it, overshadow everything we stand for? Oh, we **can** do better, and we **must** do better.

Our society is based upon "the pursuit of happiness." We have designed labels for different ideals and different agendas which have only led to animosity, lies, corruption, racism, and religious intolerance. This is not what the Founding Fathers intended when they decided to construct our Declaration of Independence and our Constitution. Our nation was built upon ideals giving birth to a unified nation; but right now, people have a distorted image of our political parties. We are living, working, and functioning in broken-ness. We are *splintered*.

Chapter Two

The Bus is Real

Have you heard the phrase, "throwing you under the bus?" Well, let me share some shocking news with you. ***The bus is real.***

I researched the phrase, "throwing you under the bus" and it has many meanings. I assure you that I am not describing the long motor vehicle used for carrying passengers, usually along a fixed route. Though what happens after being *thrown under the bus,* is a route some choose to follow.

For the sake of this chapter, I am talking about the following two definitions:

Definition #1: sacrificing others for personal or political gain
Definition #2: taking ownership for something you have not done, so you can look good

Hence, are we sacrificing, throwing America under the bus, for political gain? Unlike the vehicular bus, there are no stop signs, yield signs, or red lights to slow down, proceed with caution, or stop men and women who will cause havoc in your life to get to the top or to be elevated among their peers. Regardless of the color or the model of the bus, it (the bus) is real and there is someone waiting (a *bus extraordinaire*) that will not only throw you under the bus, but will excitedly and purposely lay you down, put the bus in drive or reverse, and run it right smack over you without blinking an eye. You know what? Many of you may have already been thrown under the bus without even realizing.

Friends, who use you as a pawn in their game, are throwing you under the bus.

Ask yourself, " Have I been thrown?"

Example #1: You are encouraged by the powers-that-be to run for an office in their club. Truth be told, they would rather have someone else and are actively campaigning against you. So, why did they ask you? They asked you because they know that there are others, whom they fear winning, will not run if your name is on the ballot. *Uh-oh, you have just been thrown under the bus.*

24

Example #2: You painfully watch someone mesmerize an audience with information gained from an event where you spoke about how to make things better for a community; you spoke on the subject because you had actually done the things you suggested for others to implement in their own communities. Interestingly, you hear your plan being delivered to this larger group by someone claiming to be close to you who has not done these things, but now feels qualified to tell others how and why they should do it. Oh, by the way, they forgot to say where their plan or idea came from in the first place. *You have just been thrown under the bus.*

There is no limit to what a man or woman will do if you are standing in the way of his or her journey to fame, stardom, and political recognition. Caution, yield, set the cruise control and hang on during the ride. Better yet, get out of the lane of betrayal, and find yourself a lane that provides you a safe ride.

Do you feel like taking a test-drive today?

As you can see my friends, I welcome you to the political arena where there is not only brokenness, but total distain for staying in your lane. The Army says, "be all that YOU can be." Why, then, are we mimicking others instead of finding out what is our own best self? Is your bus trying to mimic the actions of a truck or a sedan? Why should you care if the bus is real? Why is there a mention of a bus at all? Can we, as Americans, simply play in our own backyard and leave our neighbors backyards to our neighbors? In other words, should we carry a spare tire for emergencies, since those in positions of power will use their position to the detriment of others, to influence and control the lives of others.

Bizarre as it may seem, politics even has its own Hurricane bus. Get out of the eye of the storm, because just when everything appears calm and peaceful, the *Hurricane bus* will hit with more force than ever. It is pitiful and pathetic, but oh, so real.

The bus is real, and you must be the determiner of whether or not it will run over you.

Chapter Three

Why Didn't We Listen?

by: Mack Curry III (Trey)

What if I told you that your world, your reality, was nothing more than a dream, a fantasy based upon someone else's desire? Normally, something as provocative as that would catch peoples' attention and drive them to understand why their life is not a true existence but a figment of their imagination. What if, instead, I told you that your world was actually true in every color, physical sensation, mental stimulation, and construct that could be interpreted by the five main senses? Now it is less interesting, because you no longer have the doubt or fear that life is not what it seems or appears to be, but is exactly as it comes without deviation from the plan. This, however, leads me to my true question, one that is not so easily answered without careful analysis and precise deliberation. Why is the social structure of the U.S. fractured by the ideals of two main political factions that create friction with each other simply because they have not realized that their end goal is the same?

There is no one right answer; there are just better than most answers, but it is because there is no "one right answer" that limits the cohesion and unity of U.S. citizens with each other. Everyone is shouting out their ideas, their principles, their goals, but no one is listening to where people agree on any of those aims. Instead of building one another up, we, as a society, are merely causing white noise and letting our country be dissolved in the process.

I will call them America's greatest presidents, many will not agree...many will... but in the aspect of importance in U.S. history they did a pretty fine job, well enough so to earn my respect as the greatest, and they are George Washington, our first president, and Abraham Lincoln, our 16th president.

Now Lincoln was a man of astronomical success during our Civil War as he stood his ground against slavery and fought for unity. He did not fight for the North to become more entwined with brotherly love, or for the South to become more enticed for equal rights, but solely for unity of the entire nation. Where, as a society, did we go wrong to think that Lincoln's hard fought fight for national unity meant that he wanted just a physical cohesion being that the North and South would work together for future goals? He also meant mental harmony of every citizen so that we might aspire to achieve greatness, together, and not one party being in command over the other or one person taking full charge while others crawl in their wake. Are we honestly going to say that Lincoln did not want full congruity but was willing to lose his presidency, lose his home, endanger his family, and risk his life just for the North and the South to communicate and do business, surely not, and it is almost an insult to his memory that we have not tried to take his legacy and finish out his wishes like he had intended to do before his assassination. Yes, we were able to complete most of them, but it was the fundamental principles of life that were originally hard wired into our brain, from birth, that he had expected us to grasp and be able to do on our own without needing someone to tell us how to do it. Lincoln freed men, Sam Colt made men equal, but who will be the one to rise up and guide our nation to apposition, or did we just miss them? Did we collectively ignore the biggest act for our nation simply because we like the idea of having separate political systems to cater to the ideas of everyone, or is it because we are human and fear change and evolution?

Washington warned us, gave us clear instructions, and yet we did not listen to the only president to ever get 100 percent of the Electoral College votes in the election.

"I have already intimated to you the danger of parties in the State, with particular reference to the founding of them on geographical discriminations. Let me now take a more comprehensive view, and warn you in the most solemn manner against the baneful effects of the spirit of party generally...," text straight from Washington's farewell address as he declined running in the election again and was trying to teach us a solid lesson. *"Political parties will be the death of our nation and it is within all the corruption, the deceit, and the slander that our nation will become as dull as a butter knife and as fragile as silence."* Some parties have fallen off the roster because they lost support, circumstance, lost the running, lost members, or simply forgot what they stood for; but, there are too many that still remain today and the ones that have transcended time and become the true danger to U.S. congruity, are the Republican Party and the Democratic Party. A 100 percent vote was not enough to stop the creation of these two parties and Lincoln's ideals could not persuade the people to dissolve the parties and form invariability, so what will stop the disease for which political parties are plaguing the nation? What will cause people to stop fighting with each other simply because their party asks it of them or because they do not agree with ideas of their neighbor and the guy down the block? People of the U.S., and of the world, understand that being alone will get you far in life as you rely on no one to do what you need to do, but how far can you get in life when you lose your reason for living it. Let me rephrase that for anyone that did not understand what I said. You, and yes I am talking directly to the reader of this chapter whoever you may be, king, pauper, pope, atheist, lawyer, beggar, it does not matter who you are, or your title, you are still a human and restrained by human limitations and I will tell you how far you get in life depends solely upon your will; but imagine when your will breaks and you have given all that you have to give. What will you do then? In the perfect society where we all can agree upon one goal and work different jobs to achieve it together, you will not have to worry about that for when your will breaks and you are tired, there will be someone to pat you on the back, tell you how well you did and how much stronger you have gotten, and will put your arm over their shoulder, LIFT you up, and keep walking with you to that goal, for you have not given everything you have until you are six-feet under. If you are still breathing, you have some carbon dioxide to give to the world. If your heart is beating, you have some blood you can give to someone. If your muscles are trembling, it is because they are excited to see how much more they can take, how much more they can grow before they break or fall off. You can only get so far alone in a world meant for partnership, for cooperation, for unity, for stability. A house is not stable on one piece of wood, but on several floor boards mixed with tons of concrete and iron. So why, do we as a nation, think our country can be stable when we are having hung juries, when our Congress cannot decide on a bill because half believe it is valid while the other half believes it is not, when our president is biased to one side because of his or her political beliefs and has very little interest in what the other side is saying? I went from a lot of people to one person and the problem still links to having different beliefs than the person next to you, and political parties are not trying to fix these problems but making the separation larger. We have news networks that openly tell people whether they are conservative or liberal. How much more bias do we need to see before we are willing to change the principles on which the united, UNITED States of America focuses? What has to happen for us to gain enough intelligence, every single person, to comprehend that our nation has been *splintered* by the burden political parties has placed on us, to assimilate, to betray, and to disregard our fellow brethren all because our party is different than their own. Our first president warned us of the looming danger and we are seeing the result throughout history and more evidently so, in this day of age centuries after he wrote that message. This is dark in many regards, but I can find some humor in this all the same when I think just about the Republican Party and the Democratic Party and how they are fighting about how the nation is run. I find it more hilarious simply because if you listen closely, in this case just read, you will see that they are arguing for the nation to have the same end result.

The Republicans scream and shout for the Conservative view that the people should rule the nation, that the people should govern themselves without the atrocity of a central government powering over them like Big Brother. The Democrats are screaming and shouting for the Liberal view that they want a strong central government with political stability and public support in place over the nation... but that is where people stop listening, and where they stop reading. Catch this right now, the last words of the Conservative statement are: so that it can guide and teach the U.S. citizens how to be able to rule themselves and think collectively for the same goals and to rid the presence of a Big Brother figure from occurring and powering over them. They want the same goal but in a different time frame is all, so the real argument is not on the outcome of the nation but on when the people are ready to govern themselves. If you think they are ready now, I would say you are a Republican, and if you think they still need to learn, I would say you are a Democrat, but let me ask everyone this. Until we learn to think as one unit and move together like the wind, when will we be able to decide when we are ready, and what will be the first plan of action when we have no one other than ourselves to tell us what we are doing and how? I do not enjoy the idea of being *splintered*, I want to glue this country back together right now, but I can already guess that by the time we are ready to make that decision, the next debate will be on whether we should buy super glue or gorilla glue.

We have Faith, you will Learn

If the year is 2014 and modern science gave to us the capability to bring back to life fallen bodies and reanimate their psyche allowing us to communicate with them and allowing them to respond, what would occur if we reanimated George Washington and Abraham Lincoln? Would they be proud of what we accomplished and disappointed in what we failed to recognize? Not changing their personality but allowing them to catch up with what all has occurred after their deaths, let us see them in a new light and in a *debate* as to the future of the U.S. and its political spectrum.

"THE DEBATE"

George Washington: Well, it appears to me that this fragile country did not heed my warning to dissolve all political parties and unite the nation psychologically as much as time has allowed it to unite physically.

Abraham Lincoln: Were you expecting anything less than that? The parties have given the nation adversity as much as it has fueled its progress. Without the parties, I surely would not have been elected and all the changes I made would never have occurred. Who knows what kind of madness would be plaguing the United States right now had they listened.

Washington: Let me ask you this... If we did not have political parties, how do you figure presidents, congressmen, justices, and bureaucrats would be elected or appointed to their positions?

Lincoln: I would suppose that, they would be chosen by the nation, or, rather by the electoral colleges, due to their achievements, accomplishments, titles, stature, heroism, personality, disposition...Oh, I see what you are trying to get at.

Washington: Do you now? What am I trying to have you and the rest of the nation comprehend?

Lincoln: Instead of viewing candidates for their political party, which would arbitrarily dictate their ideals and goals, we would view them for the people they are and choose people that would make the best decisions for the nation based upon their ideals and not simply the ideals of the party they are associated with. Instead of saying Federalists vote for Federalists and Anti-Federalists for Anti-Federalists, rather, Democrats and Republicans voting for their own parties because of rules, could vote openly for the right person for the job. I understand that, but let me ask you a question now. How could we truly find the right person for the job? There are billions of people on this continent alone. How can we find "the one"?

Washington: You are correct. Without the parties, "the one" cannot be simply nominated by the party, but let us also remember this...the best person for the job is not always nominated by the party to run; as a matter of fact, most of the time, or at least as I have read in these history books over the past few decades, it is who the party views will do what the party wants them to do. It is the people who will not fight for their beliefs but will comply with the party's agenda; those are the people the parties nominate. They forget that the nation is depending on their best judgment, not dates and times placed on a calendar in backdoor meetings without consideration for the state of being of the United States.

Lincoln: That is quite true, in every regard you stated. It is no longer a "best person gets the job" type of system, more like a beauty pageant or a race to see who can brownnose the most, first. Alright, so I will go with you and say that political parties are dissolving the nation and choosing the wrong people for the most important jobs. How would you fix the problem, because this has been a way of life for centuries, and not all change is beneficial?

Washington: As I was peering over all that I have missed due to my death, I came across some very interesting and insightful people. One of those people was a man named Morgan Freeman. First off, let me commemorate you for your accomplishments during your term and I thank you for saving the nation during the Civil War.

Lincoln: Thank you. That coming from you is a truly great honor to be recognized, but I cannot take all the credit. The citizens of this nation wanted the change and unity as much as I did, they just had different opinions on how it should be achieved and run.

Washington: Indeed so, but carrying on with my point, Morgan Freeman had an interview, on "television" of course seeing as how people only pay attention to things broadcast on this "television" or on these things called "cell phones" and internet with things called Facebook and Twitter; even a place called an Instagram, but naturally it was on television and not in a newspaper or a letter. During this interview Mr. Freeman was asked how he would end racism, and his response astounded me. I never thought anyone, especially an elderly Black man, would say what he said knowing the atrocious history of racism America was founded from. He said, in response to the question, "Stop talking about it".

Lincoln: Stop talking about it? How can we stop talking about it? Our greatest legacies were born and brought forth from it. How can I forget what I cannot forgive? It is like discarding your history. Forgetting one's history will doom them to repeat their mistakes, from the past, in the future. It's so foolish. It will not work, but hurt the nation more.

Washington: I know you are very emotional on this subject, but listen and think about his words carefully. He said "stop talking about it", because he understands what most people, including yourself, have a tough time trying to comprehend.

Lincoln: Oh, and what is that?

Washington: If people were to stop identifying each other as any color other than "gray", we would not see each other as all that different. I mean to say, if you were not White and he was not Black, but both of you were gray, you would not recognize yourself as those distinguishing features like black or white, but instead you would just interpret yourselves as both being men. If I did not see you as a Republican or a Democrat, a Federalist or an Anti-Federalist, or any political denomination, I would just see you as a man, another man just like myself, and I would judge you only as a man you carried yourself to be and your actions would determine my opinion of you.

Lincoln: I... I see what you are saying. We are so hung up on hatred, differences, and violence that we keep bringing up the pain of the past, the differences in appearance, and the variety of ideals that we forget to think and count on what is truly important in this world.

It truly would be a better world if everything was gray, the color that lies between the two most opposite points. The point where color is neither rejected nor consumed, where it is not all there, nor is it void, where it is neither filthy, nor is it pure. It is the border of realms, and the perfect state of being. If we stop talking about racism and identify ourselves as people rather than by color, racism will end for their will be no virtue, no structure, no perseverance in it because no one can be racist without races existing. Thus, with this logic, if there are no political parties to join, we are forced to pick people that stand out among the rest because of what they do, by their actions.

Thus, we will not be so easily preyed upon by false promises and forsaken words, but rather we could see the changes actually occur and come from the people who are willing to make the changes themselves. You are also right, in the fact, that it is astonishing a Black man, after all the pain and suffering his race has gone through in the past, is willing to forget all of that and make all the children of this world and those to come, be ignorant to it so that the world can move forward and all the racism will die in the past just like it should have long ago.

I guess what everyone missed was that *"not everything can be equal if we view them as different to begin with"*. How can we say all men are created equal and fight for equal rights if we are fighting for the equal rights of Black people, Latinos, Asians, Native Americans, and so forth? How can we say all men are created equal if we are constantly calling them by that name rather than saying we are fighting for the equal treatment of that "human being", of "that person", of "that body"?

In my Gettysburg Address, I said, "that government of the people, by the people, for the people, shall not perish from the earth." I did not say for a specific color, for a specific race, for a specific background, for a specific party, for a specific ideal, but of ALL PEOPLE, THE people, of this nation which hath given life and purpose to this government. Even I forgot what I stood for, now I understand why they did not listen… it is because they could not, because we were blinded by the borders we created within our own minds.

Washington: Our time here is done good sir, our minds cannot stay on this plane for any longer now. I am so pleased to witness you comprehending what I meant in my final address and what it appears Mr. Freeman meant in his statement. Perhaps someone will see this debate and pay attention to it completely and come to the same under-standing you have. This nation will do well, very well indeed, as long as they listen this time and are willing to make the necessary change needed to obtain the full potential this beautiful nation was designed to achieve. I have faith in them, do you?

Lincoln: I barely had faith in myself and I was able to see it; so, I am quite positive that the children of this generation will be able to acquire this knowledge and grow from it. You are right; the potential is there, but the change is required to achieve it.

Chapter Four

A Republican Party Revival

By: Nicholas Buford

Currently, our party sits in a tough spot. Most importantly, our nation is in a tough spot. Many Americans are giving up on politics. Citizens cannot trust their elected officials to fulfill their campaign promises. Our nation's debt continues to grow. More businesses are closing doors due to a rough economy. Americans continue to get frustrated with the state of the economy and drop out of the work force. Terrorist organizations across the globe ramp up their attacks on innocent lives. America walks away from the hand of Jesus into a more secular state. Crime levels spike throughout America's cities. A justice system supposedly built on "equality" proves to be anything but equal to many young people of color. Generations of families continue to go through the cycle of poverty. Scandals plague our nation's capital. Too many still judge other humans on the "color of their skin instead of the content of their character." Political relations between the two political parties remain toxic, which stalls progress for the American people. These are the obvious issues and there are still countless more.

Right now in America, both parties are failing the people on one issue or another. Neither party has a perfect past, neither is perfect today, nor ever will be perfect. When I chose the Republican Party a few years ago, I did it after much thought and prayer. I was highly interested in politics and public service. I made the decision to look heavily into the platforms and histories of the party. I did not chose the GOP because of who was in the party, or because I agreed with every single one of its statements from party officials. I chose the party, because my views on the issues align stronger with the Republicans. When I thought about my faith, my family, the value of life, work and so much more there was no comparison. At the same time while choosing the party, I knew that the party had tons of work to do before even coming close to being perfect. I think when choosing to join the Republican Party, I felt the way (it is said)

Condoleezza Rice did when she joined. Dr. Rice did not simply join the GOP because her father was a Republican. Many may know that her father, John Rice, joined the party when the Democrats in Alabama would not allow him to register to vote…and the local Republicans did allow him to register to vote. At the 2000 Republican National Convention, Dr. Rice stated, "I joined the party for different reasons (than my father). I joined the party that sees me as an individual instead of a part of a group. I found a party that puts family first. I found a party that has a love of liberty at its core, and I found a party that believes that peace begins with strength." The same things Dr. Rice looked for in a party are what I found in the GOP.

Sometimes, I think if the Republican Party forgets where it came from, it will lose control of its future. The Republican Party was founded in Wisconsin, in 1854, on the simple platform of freeing the slaves. The scholars can argue whether Lincoln, before the Presidency, was against slavery in general or just against the spread of it. However, there is no debate when it comes to the fact that the Republican, President Lincoln, delivered the 1863 Emancipation Proclamation that called for freedom of all the enslaved population across America. Let us not forget that the Republican Party pushed the 13th, 14th, and 15th Amendments into existence. The GOP was the party for the first dozens of elected Black congressional officials. In addition, Republicans set up the Freedman's Bureau and other government programs to assist freed slaves as they entered into citizenship and private life. These reconstruction pro-grams were not a "hand-out." They were a "hand-up" to citizens who were finally starting to be treated like citizens, although not in every regard. Republicans must know that the party's actions in the 19th century were not about libera-lism or big government. The actions were built on freedom and the thought that these citizens should have their rights protected as well. Many Republicans know these actions and will quote them simply as facts. However, these are more than facts; they are the starting platform and legislation of one of America's political parties. If the party forgets this, more elections will be lost and more people will fade away.

Today, many citizens view the Republican Party as old, "out of touch," and unpopular. Yet, there are many ways that the party can resurge and win big again. Look at the state of the country, states, and cities. They face huge problems. Many who vote for Democrats will admit that the Democratic Party's solutions are not creating over-whelming solutions at all. There are many, especially young people, who hope to have a thriving political environment where both parties fight for every vote based on issues and platforms, not rhetoric. In this regard, the Republican Party can step up to the plate. It does not require changing values and adopting the plan of the Democrats. However, it does require understanding the issues that Americans do and do not face today. It requires being bold enough to create solutions that will work and push those solutions to every voter.

I say it's time for the party to have a revival. Revival is defined as "an improvement in the condition and the strength of something." When I discuss with people the direction our party should go, I like to use the term "contemporary conservatism." The term contemporary means "living or occurring at the same" and "belonging or occurring in the present." This is what the party must under-stand. The GOP does not have to go through an extrava-gant change of its platform to win again. Today, the Republican Party promotes faith, freedom, and capitalism. The party can experience a revival and be contemporary while still standing for faith, freedom, and capitalism. The party must understand how this relates to today's time and the battles that America faces today. Understanding how this relates to today can lead to that revival, growth, and victory of the party.

Our country is in strong need of revival. Many can see the culture change continuing to drift away from Christ. Yes, I think people should be able to choose their own religion or be able to choose not to worship at all if they like. However, if our pledge of allegiance says we are "one nation under God," shouldn't we act like it? We often say "God Bless America," but how can we expect Him to bless our nation while we're so disobedient to Him? Americans cannot forget the role that faith played in our country's history. Think about Great Awakenings that occurred throughout the colonies that led people to understanding the Word of God. Think about war generals praying for their men and the favor of the Lord before heading into battle during the Revolution-ary War. Think about the role faith played in the lives of American slaves as they prayed to Christ day-in and day-out that freedom may be reached someday. Think about the churches and religious organizations that organized and rallied citizens during the push for Civil Rights and Voting Rights in the 1950s and 1960s. Think about the family mem-bers that pray every night for their loved one in America's uniform to return home safely. There is a need for more "awakenings" across our country. Churches across America must rise up and work to lead others to Christ across our nation. Yes, I think doing missions in third world countries is great. Yet, there are millions right here in America that des-perately need to hear the Gospel. They need to hear the message of the true Savior, the man who can make a way out of no way.

There needs to be a party in America that stands up for God's word. However, standing closer is not enough. The party must stand for the full word of Christ and not back down against those attempts to push Christ away. The Re-publican Party has long been pro-life. However, we must understand that being pro-life does not just mean "in the womb." The party must stand for life from conception all the way to natural death. That means standing for citizens' rights, all of their rights, until death. What citizens look like, where citizens come from, or what the citizens' last name is does not make them any less than a citizen. The Word tells us that Christ loves all of His children and that each one is special within His sight. One of my favorite verses is Galatians 1:15 that states, "God sets us apart in our mother's womb and calls us by His amazing grace." The battle for life is still contemporary, just as it was in 1973, and Republicans must keep it at the forefront. Republicans must promote pro-life policies across our country, while at the same time promoting adoption. We need to also be the "pro-adoption" party. Let's work so everyone sees the value in human life and every child can have a family and a home.

Today, America sees a rise in the number of states that are passing pro-gay marriage legislation. The Word is clear that marriage is between "one man and one woman." While people may call Republicans out-of-touch, standing for God's definition of marriage is right. Republicans can be against gay marriage while still not being "bigots" to those members of the LGBT community. Making sure those citizens are not discriminated against in universities, workplaces, and other areas is pivotal. That's standing up for liberty, freedom, and the rights of all. Americans cannot forget who created marriage in the first place. God created marriage, not the government. The government cannot redefine something that it had no hand in creating. The Republican Party must rally people of faith to stand up for traditional marriage. At the same time, the party has to defend the basic, constitutional rights of all citizens.

"Liberty and justice for all" is a key theme of our country's pledge of allegiance. As a party that fights for freedom, the GOP must defend the rights of each citizen.

America's justice system is in dire need of reform. The American judicial system penalizes young citizens of color more heavily than it does others. This is not an opinion; it is fact. It is also an injustice. It's not as though people of color are doing crimes more outrageous than anyone else. The system heavily bends towards tougher sentencing for people of color. At the same time, police forces in cities across the country discriminate in actions towards people of color. While some in the Democratic party talk about defending rights and being for minority voters, they are not putting meaningful proposals on the table to reform America's justice system. Meanwhile, there are Republicans who are starting to put proposals on the table. The plans to reform the justice system cannot just remain "proposals", they must become law. Too many citizens are pushed into long term imprisonment due to wacky mandatory minimum laws. After hearing how long some have served in jail for some crimes, you will begin to scratch your head and know something is wrong.

Mandatory minimum laws must be reformed. Reforming mandatory minimum sentencing can save money to invest into re-entry and job training programs. Even more important than that, it is time to restore voting rights for non-violent felons. One would be surprised how many citizens, especially Black males, cannot vote due to a non-violent felony charge. I think it's outrageous that someone's voting rights can be stripped away for smoking pot. To have a country that truly stands on 'liberty and justice for all',

America must have a justice system that treats each citizen with justice and respect, while at the same time giving proper and common-sense punishment for those who break the law. Reforming a broken judicial system is one of the civil rights issues of the 21st century.

Education is still a key that can unlock many doors. It is a tragedy that today, in America, you can tell whether a child attends a good school by looking at their zip code. Too many children are attending failing schools. However, money continues to flow to failing schools year after year. Most times, children living in poverty are most affected by this. Each child should have access to a quality education. The government should remove any blockades that stand in the way of children receiving a quality education. In fact, government should promote educational opportunity. The Republican Party must push for every parent to at least have a choice of sending their child to a better school. School funding needs to follow children's interest not the schools. Yes, school choice is pivotal. However, school choice is not about ripping money from public schools. Public schooling is excellent, when the school is succeeding. Public schools are excellent, when children learning are put first. We need a nation when every child, regardless of color, last name, or zip code can attend a great school. It does not matter if the school is public, private, charter, magnet, religious, or any other. Republican governors should open up access to better schools for families, especially the poor. Children should be the first priority. A strong education means a better chance at continuing learning after high school graduation. Improving education is one step in ending the cycles of poverty that many families deal with in America today.

I often say that Capitalism has done more to rescue people from poverty than any other economic system on Earth. It's capitalism that has moved people from poverty into the middle class. Our country must continue to be one based on free enterprise. The spirit of free enterprise must be spread across the nation in a way that its benefits can transform communities. Never underestimate the power of entrepreneurship. America's entrepreneurs take big risks for something that starts out as an idea. Promoting small business ownership is crucial to reviving the economy. Our government needs to get some regulations out of the way that hurt small business owners. Too many regulations lead entrepreneurs to lay off workers, eliminate business locations, or close the business overall. Yes, there needs to be some business regulations that protect the American workforce and the economic state of the country. However, today, too many regulations pile up on business owners. We need more business owners. America is in need for more business owners in all states and communities. Yet, small business ownership numbers cannot grow if the environment for owning a business is not favorable. This is especially important for areas of a high minority population. This, too, is a way to combat poverty. I recently read how the Ohio state government, under the leadership of Governor John Kasich, is now setting state records for the amount of small business loans that are going to Black business owners. Investing in Black businesses helps urban and rural communities. It leads to a lower unemployment rate among Blacks, and it leads to more paychecks being handed out to citizens who need them. Promoting small business ownership is a pillar of the GOP today and this effort must penetrate outside of areas that are under GOP control. A message must be sent to urban areas, that entrepreneurship opens opportunity and creates more jobs.

The economic revival does not stop at just investing more in business owners. Setting up economic empower-ment zones in places of high poverty is of high importance. Economic empowerment zones promote stable community growth. These empowerment zones attempt to uplift com-munities for longer than a set period of time. These com-munities need long-term community based policies that will impact families. A proposal for setting up economic empow-erment zones must provide tax credits for minority business owners, tax incentives for the citizens who cooperate within the scope of the community partnerships, and investments in keeping energy costs low for these high poverty areas. America needs the "all of the above" energy strategy that some politicians talk about. When energy costs go up, it hurts the poor more than any other group. By setting up an economic empowerment zone, in addition to school choice and investments in minority business, owners will prove to be very beneficial in resurrecting the economies of urban cities.

Even with the above stated economic reforms, America is in awful need of tax reform. The American tax code is too old and too complex. Most Americans cannot understand the tax code. The tax code is also full of loopholes that benefit white collar citizens that do not need loopholes. I'm sure most Republicans and Democrats can agree we need tax reform. Our tax code needs to be simpler and much fairer. I would propose eliminating all of the complex personal tax brackets down to two brackets. My idea would be a 15% bracket and a 30% bracket that's broken down by income levels. That's debatable. Some would suggest going to one bracket around 20%. That is debatable as well. The key objective in tax reform should be making sure it is simpler and more fair. Tax reform should not hurt business owners or those in poverty. Our nation needs more tax payers, not less. A growth in jobs equals a growth in paychecks. That leads to more people putting into the tax system. Common sense tax reform means getting rid of loopholes for those who do not need them. Allowing more family tax credits to the personal income tax should also be a part of reform. The personal income tax is not the lone part of the tax code that needs to be fixed. Currently, America has the highest corporate tax in the world. Think about all the jobs that are sent oversees simply due to our corporate tax rate. It's time to compete with other countries in terms of this high tax rate, and promote more jobs coming to America.

Our nation's overall economic shape needs to be adjusted. The government must stop spending more money than it takes in, and start moving towards a balanced budget. Government officials need to take bold steps in eliminating wasteful spending to get America closer to a balanced budget. This will require making tough choices when it comes to reforming government programs. Some government programs need reform, not elimination. Our welfare system is one area that needs to be reformed. America needs a welfare system in place to assist citizens in a time of need. However, this system of welfare should be a safety net. There's a difference between a safety net and a hammock. The safety net helps citizens while they work towards the rebound. A hammock is something you lie in all day and in terms of welfare, it can become generational. Some citizens are now at an age, where due to the times when they grew up, government assistance is needed to help them. It is a "hand-up" and not a "hand-out." Yet, for those now at their prime in the 21st century, generational poverty should not be acceptable. Truth is (despite what some elected officials will tell you), most families do not want to be on welfare. Most people on welfare do not want to live off of the government. Look around, the situation is getting worse. What do you see? You see more people going into poverty, more businesses shutting down, towns degrading, and more children attending failing schools. This is where *the we* must tie in school choice, entrepreneurship, economic empowerment zones, keeping energy cost low, and tax reform to help crush poverty from its roots. Binding together policies that uplift individuals from the grips of poverty need to be a top priority of a contemporary GOP.

Ever since the Declaration of Independence was signed, foreign policy has been of importance to the direction of our nation. America has the best military in the world. It must remain that way. Our men and women volunteer and leave their families and fight for our country and freedom. There's a huge debate whether America should meddle in international conflicts or isolate from the world. I think there is a way America can lead the world on the international front, while not isolating or meddling in every conflict across the globe. America must continue to lead the world, because so many nations look to us as what they aspire to be. However, it is past time to cut off foreign aid to many countries across the globe, many whom do not operate in the best interest of freedom. Regardless of the year or the conflict, America's military must be well-funded and well-prepared. Our military must be at a status where other nations are too afraid to test us. Our leaders must be bold and articulate enough to keep America respected across the world stage.

All of the objectives above are some of the stances the GOP must take to be a better party. Above that, Republicans must take a message of growth and opportunity to every individual. Every citizen wants a thriving economy, great schools, low energy costs, a strong military, and a nation that protect his or her rights. Race, gender, income level, region, and more does not matter. In most cases, there is more that unites Americans than divides them. Others, to include the media, will not make it seem that way. They always want class warfare, race warfare, battles, and drama. America is better than that. America deserves better than that. Conservatives across the nation must rally together behind common sense principles and common sense leaders that stand for ideals that will uplift and empower citizens. There is a growing group of people who want the GOP to be revived again and compete with the Democratic Party. This is very true within the Black community. At times, I say that the Republican Party has given up on the Black vote for too long, which has caused the Black vote to give up on the GOP. There are solutions that the GOP has, to uplift and empower Black Americans with more jobs, chances to attend better schools, access to capital, and more. However, the Republican office holders and the rank-and-file who believe in those solutions, must prevail against those who do not. In order to win America, the Republican Party has to look like America. This means hiring more diverse staff, promoting a more diverse slate of candidates, launching marketing campaigns to each area of the country, and promoting policies that open up doors of opportunity to those who need it most. Meanwhile, conservatives must end the bitterness after primary fights, and line up behind party nominees. When November comes, there are only two choices. In order to get America on the right track, one party has to put an end to the bickering and start offering solutions. The Republican Party can be that party. The party must not forget how it organized in the first place and what led to victory. The Republican Party can be revived and win big again. It will take the right vision, the right leaders, and sticking to the Word while having faith in Almighty God.

Chapter Five

▶Are You Supporting a Pyramid or a Totem Pole?

by: Nakeisha M. Curry, M.D.

Our Founding Fathers established a nation meant to provide freedom and democracy for all of its citizens. In their original model, the political structure was built in the shape of a pyramid. Everyone was viewed as an important member of society whose presence was vital for the stability of the structure. Even if you were at the top of the pyramid, there was an underlying respect for those who were "beneath you". You realized that, without a strong base or foundation, your position at "the top" would soon fall. When you looked down, you saw the faces of the strong faithful men and women who supported you. Even though you may not have always agreed with everyone, you respected everyone as an equal, with an equal voice. You put your differences aside, because you realized that if even one person didn't succeed, EVERYONE failed. In fact, in this model, the people "on the bottom" were the most vital members. If they failed to carry their own weight, the entire structure crumbled to the ground. Therefore, you adopted philosophies like, "All for one and one for all," "It takes a village," and "United we stand."

Somehow, somewhere along our journey, we lost our way. The base of our pyramid began to narrow until our structure changed into a totem pole. We now have a society that focuses only on the person at the top. Now, you have no respect for or even acknowledgement of the people "beneath you". When you look down, you don't see any faces. This is because, everyone lines up vertically: each one with his/her head up his/her superior's derriere. With this positioning, the only voice you hear belongs to the person on top. Therefore, you create a disloyal organization without integrity whereby each member will do anything to achieve the top spot. If people don't carry their own weight, it matters not. There will always be someone else willing to insert his/her head where yours once was. You begin to adopt philosophies like, "There are no rules in love and war,"

"Low man on the totem pole," and "By whatever means necessary."

Why is this structural transition important? Because both are successful. Both have the ability to prosper. However, one builds successful cohesive societies while the other *splinters* them. The truth is that we all matter and are created equally, but we have been trained and brainwashed to believe that we don't matter and are not equal. You must decide for yourself where you belong. It's time to pull your head out. Stop just looking up and spend some time looking around. You might just find the other members of your structure who have been waiting for you to step into place, united, to repair the *splinters* of your life, and restore the freedom and democracy that your Founding Fathers fought so bravely for you to enjoy.

Chapter Six

Educational Policies/Broken Pieces?

by: Ashante Y. Everett

Educational policies like the No Child Left Behind Act (NCLB) and the American Recovery Act (ARRA) were based on the premises of setting high standards, establishing measurable goals, raising achievement, and producing better results for children and young people (Education, 2008) (Education, 2009). These policies are contingent upon students meeting required outcomes on standardized tests and turning around low-performing schools. By meeting these standards, students are given opportunities to compete with other students across the states. This is critical for students who move from one state to another and for students who look outside of their state for college and career opportunities. These policies are also instrumental in holding teachers accountable to teaching the required curriculum and making educational progress. The positive effects of these policies are reflected in the increased U.S. graduation rate and the increased number of highly qualified teachers. This sounds like a win-win situation for our students and reflects a moment for our nation to take a bow. Unfortunately, while we were taking a bow and vowing to leave no children behind, we left all children behind...behind, on a *splintered* path causing them to become scratched and bruised on their journeys.

Educational policies seem to be accompanied by ideas of unreachable measures and unwarranted pressures on teachers. In many cases, pressures of educational policies and the demand for increased student achievement and teacher effectiveness, have led to teachers forgetting about students, and concentrating on ways to beat the system. The same system that was created to protect our students turned into the system that destroyed our students.

In this new system, students have assumed the roles of pawns in the school system's game of chess. High achievers are moved to the side for average achievers who are moved to the front by under achievers. These achievers are now known by numbers on an Excel sheet instead of by names on a roster. When this happens, it becomes easy for some to lose track of reality.

The new reality goes back to making sure the numbers are high by any means necessary. Numbers determine worth, which determines jobs. These jobs have some playing their part in a broken system.

Broken systems have been played out like a soap opera on our local news channels. Instead of watching the "Young and the Restless," I chose to watch "The Cheaters of School System X," a real life scandal that implicated educators in a cheating scheme that spanned several years. A real-life scandal that reinforced to our parents and children the unimportance of education. A real life scandal that had many believe that a superior led her administrative teams in scandalous behavior in order to meet the demands of educational policies and gain rewards associated with these policies. A real life scandal where the scenes will outlive the characters.

When the final scene closes on this act, I wonder if the risks were worth the rewards. I wonder if the real life soap opera should have held a casting call for others. I wonder if the superior should have really been the main character. I wonder if any of this will matter in five years.

Over the past few years, many people opposed to educational policies shared in the beliefs that the educational system has left every child behind with the introduction of the No Child Left Behind Act. School systems witnessed the stress from teachers and parents associated with high-stakes tests and the demand for highly qualified teachers. Teachers, in many instances, stopped teaching children and relied on only teaching a test. In other instances, schools maximized the number of students in each class in order for those students to be taught by a highly qualified teacher, a teacher who earned this status by checking the appropriate boxes on an application...all for the sake of meeting the demands of educational policies and mandates.

Conversely, educational policies have served our educational system in positive ways; for the influences of these policies have provided students with opportunities for the future while crushing their hopes for today. Like many great things in our society, educational policies will continue to help educational progress while hindering our educational system. In these educational systems, one will find that at the root of the policies are individual philosophies and selfish priorities.

Philosophies educate me on nothing more than the person behind the philosophy. May I introduce you to Philo Sophia? If so, you will meet the passion behind the push.

My passions force me to wake up cheering for educational policies and mandates and go to bed crying for our children. I stand firm on leveling the playing field for all students, while I watch the gap widen between students. I support teachers with research-based instructional strategies, but I question the motives behind the research. I wrote this with passion; consequently, I am subjected to abomination.

As those turn against me and change their minds about me, our society changes and changes again. As society changes, so do the structures and values held in the educational system. If those familiar with the history of education were to look at the school system today, they would render many questions. These questions would be about where the educational system is headed and how long this *splintered* journey will take.

On my journey, I just found that scrutinizing educational policies, mandates, and laws is clearly not the answer. I no longer want to look past my reflection; I will eventually see my reflection. I will not take your leftovers; my existence was not my choice. I do not want a solution for my failure; I want an opportunity to succeed. I want educational policies to be grounded in the interest of our students; I will carry a file on my journey until the road becomes smooth.

66

Chapter Seven

Who is the Highest Bidder?

by: Ashante Y. Everett

As I look to conquer my next task, I wonder how I will approach the endeavor and with how much tenacity; what determines these two things are the motives in which I have driving my actions. Fortunately, for me, integrity and character drive all of my actions. Because of this, when I am asked to join a project or accompany a team, the motivation for me is because of me. Once I join, I am self-motivated and unwavered by any foolishness, any corruption, or any judgment that may transpire. I wish I could say the same for others. For if we all seek to accomplish the goals from a place that requires us to know our space, this splintered road we travel will become smooth.

My space, me, here, did not get here because of you; me, growing, will happen in spite of you. This notion, me, unattached from you, often perplexes others. It leaves them wondering, "Who are you?"

On the contrary, the question should not be, "Who are you?" The question should be, "Whose are you?" This question should be asked sparingly; not everyone is prepared to answer. I send a warning to those who want to know the answer and caution them to wait until they are fully prepared to answer.

For example, start with your current position. Did you get this position by making a promise you now wish you didn't have to keep? If so, the answer is, you do not belong to yourself. You do not belong to yourself because someone bought you. Consequently, the cost for yourself was a measly position you could have attained with hard work, dedication, and faith. If you felt the only way for you to have gotten that position was to sell yourself, I must then ask, "Is that the position you really wanted?" If the answer is yes, I then ask you, "Why did you sell yourself to the lowest bidder?"

With high stakes and low bids, we find ourselves in a constant state of confusion. The under-qualified and over-rated sitting next to someone highly-qualified and under estimated. Meetings are no longer based on work, but are now based on trust; no longer based on supporting the mission, but creating a perception; no longer hitting targets, but dodging bullets. All of this at what cost?

The cost is now based on who you know, not what you know, and the price is to stay in it, to win it, or be executed. A supervisor once told me, "Sometimes you have to build them up, just to tear them down." That would be great if we were discussing trees; things that can still be of worth once torn down. But, we are talking about human lives. These lives have families that can be destroyed in the deforestation process. All of this destruction is done to divert from the incompetencies and injustices going on during the bidding wars. Once you stop selling yourself, you are free to be yourself. Once you start being yourself, will you recognize yourself? Once you can no longer recognize yourself, will you like yourself?

Being yourself is not always easy and never seems fair. However, in my life, I am sure about a few things. I may not have your bio, but I own my life. I may not have an introduction, but my work speaks for itself. I may only have a few accolades, but I earned the ones I have and made it possible for you to receive yours. These things alone should let you know who I am and lead to whose I am. For some, this question is no longer important because they cannot comprehend the notion of the me separate from you.

Do you still want to know who I am? If so, please wait until I am finished. For when I am finished, you will know exactly who I am. You can read all about me if you are willing to take the time to read my life story. Fortunately, that will probably take far too much of your time. But if you had, you would know that I was sold to the highest bidder who is saying, "Well done, my good and faithful servant." So, if you really want to know who I am and why you can't help make me, learn whose I am and know His work has already been done.

What happens when you lose your script?

Chapter Eight

≋The Hypocritical Oath

by Nakeisha Curry, M.D.

I swear by Apollo, the healer, Asclepius, Hygieia, and Panacea, and I take to witness all the gods, all the goddesses, to keep according to my ability and my judgment, the following Oath and agreement:

...I will prescribe regimens for the good of my patients according to my ability and my judgment and never do harm to anyone... (English translation of Hippocratic Oath)

As a physician, I am honored, humbled, and grateful to have been accepted into an elite group of gifted individuals

71

chosen as the guardians of human health and life. One of our most sacred principles is that of *Primum non nocere* which is a Latin phrase meaning "first, do no harm." The pioneers of medicine realized that medical practice is just as much an art as it is a science. To that end, they depended on sound moral judgment, skill, and compassion to form the foundation of their medical decisions and interventions. However, I doubt that the pioneers realized that one day government would use politics to interfere with and supersede their goals.

I guess the real question is, "Who has the right to run medicine?" Who should be in charge of the variables that affect your healthcare: access, costs, providers, etc...? America's answer appears to be the federal government. What a preposterous idea! Let's examine this principle using the automobile industry. Let's say that your vehicle is making an annoying noise that has been worsening over the past month. You have tried various simple remedies such as lubricants, oils, and cleaners, but the problem persists. Therefore, you decide to make an appointment with your vehicle's physician: the auto mechanic. The mechanic tells you that he will see you today. You arrive and the team asks you to describe the problem. Once you give a brief description, he performs a diagnostic test, provides you with a proposed solution and gives you an estimate of the repair costs. You grant permission and the authorized mechanic solves the car's problem. He also provides you with an opportunity to repair any other incidental problems that were detected during the examination. The mechanic has the autonomy to determine the best solution and set all of the fees (labor, parts, etc). You pay the bill and schedule a follow-up appointment for your car.

OK. Now, let's say that your knee is making an annoying noise that has been worsening over the past month. You have tried various simple remedies such as lubricants, oils, and analgesics, but the problem persists. Therefore, you decide to make an appointment with your body's mechanic: the primary care physician. The physician tells you that he can see you in a month. In the meantime, your problem continues to worsen. Once you finally obtain an appointment and arrive at the office, the team asks you to describe the problem ("What brings you here today?"). After you tell the phone operator who scheduled the appointment, front desk employee who registers you, medical assistant taking your vitals, and nurse settling you in the room, you finally meet the physician. What does he/she ask? "What brings you here today?" You give a brief description, followed by your entire past medical history, surgical history, family history, social history, medication history, etc... Then you are told that insurance authorization is required prior to providing diagnostic tests or referring you to a specialist (mechanic) who is authorized to repair the problem. The team states that you will have to schedule a follow-up appointment in two weeks after authorization is obtained. You receive a prescription for a medication to alleviate the pain, but the underlying problem is not cured. In addition, your requests to discuss other health concerns are deferred, because the current appointment can only address "the knee". You have to schedule different appointments for your other incidental ailments that were discovered during the examination. As you know, this process can extend for months, even years, before governmental red tape allows your physician to repair your problems. In addition, your physician has no autonomy over healthcare laws, so you (and they) are at the mercy of the politicians who determine the "best" solution and set all of the fees (insurance co-pays, costs and reimbursement of procedures, prescriptions, etc).

Let's put this in perspective. Are you aware that some auto mechanics charge $100/hr for labor to fix your car? This is more than some physicians receive per hour to fix you. Is your life not more valuable than your car's? However, we don't hear anyone lobbying or protesting against car labor costs. You just accept the quoted price given by the professional. In the same manner, you accept rising gasoline prices, produce prices, and entertainment prices (sporting events, movies, concerts, etc...). Have you ever asked yourself why you willingly pay $10 for a movie, $100 for a concert, $1,000 for Super Bowl tickets, and $10,000 for a car, but you don't want to spend $5 on a prescription to heal your body?

We have all been blinded, patients and physicians alike, into thinking that generalized political decisions have our best health interests at heart. How could this be allowed when they have no clinical knowledge/experience in the medical field? Physicians dedicate their lives to their patients. Just as clergy are responsible for healing your spirit, your physician is responsible for healing your body. We don't allow the government to interfere with religion (hence, separation of church and state). In the same manner, we should protect the sacred patient-physician relationship. After all, your body is a temple and should be handled with care. However, while physicians were concentrating on healing, government was concentrating on profiting. Thus, this sacred bond has been *splintered*. You have been distracted by the media and convinced that maybe, just maybe, your physician may not be your best advocate. Technology has also deceived you into feeling that everything you need to know about your health can be found online. If that were true, why do physicians undergo ten years of training (college, medical school, residency, fellowships, etc.)? Why? Because it takes that long!

When physicians make mistakes, people die. While your politicians are vacationing during their next "closed session", or your teachers are relaxing during their summer breaks, remember that your physicians are continuously on duty. However, if all of your physicians are forcefully deployed to the fight in the political arena (to protect your medical rights), who will be left to care for you when you need a doctor? We are the guardians of human health and life. Please do not allow outside forces to *splinter* the sacred patient-physician relationship. Protect your body, i.e. your temple, from all harm and danger. Entrust yourself to the chosen group of individuals who depend on sound moral judgment, skill, and compassion to form the foundation of their medical decisions and interventions. Depend on your physician, who answers to YOU: not to the local politician, billionaire, or hottest celebrity. And above all, put your medical faith in the team sworn by an oath to "first, do no harm."

Chapter Nine

■The Political Journey

by: Colonel Henry Childs (USAF retired)

I s the political plight becoming a dichotomy? The political journey is marred with struggles for freedom and equality. In either case, it would appear that America has the power to push the pendulum in either direction. Are Americans in the midst of battles for economic and political gains? The political history of most Americans is either being a Republican or a Democrat. It is rather ironic that the political journey of the Republican Party came into existence from a mutual coming together of the races. The equality and economic fate of that association resigned with the decision making of others. Fast-forward to today, where is this respect of race, gender, and religion in the political journey? Who determines the political, equality, and economic faith?

Wondering in the Political Divide

Political Scientists argue that politics involve a rationality of individual decision-making. Voters individually select candidates who articulate campaign platforms that represent the interest of voters. As such, the informed voter, based on values, morals, and beliefs, identifies with and votes for the candidate who represents the interest of the voter. The quest for political power has become a duped process of cheering and applauding. Blacks gained historical political gains during the reconstruction era. With the support of the Republican Party, they were elected to the U.S. Senate, House of Representatives, State Legislature, and State and Local political offices. Scholars conclude that more than 1,500 held office during the Reconstruction period (1865–1876); all were Republicans and accounted for the creation of platforms of protecting citizen's rights, the right to vote, racial justice, and economic equality. The voter then chose the platform as a means to achieve equal rights, racial equality, social justice, voting rights, economic liberation, and equal employment.

For the first time in American History, America became a government that contained provisions for defining and protecting civil rights. What was to follow changed history for years to come. Then, the *splintering* began.

Democrats did not go silently into the political abyss. As the northern Republicans abandoned their previous commitment to protect the rights of all citizens, the political environment returned to an American state of racial segregation and the disenfranchisement of voters.

Did the Republican Party cheer voters into the party for a primary cause to get certain ones elected to office with a collateral victory of minorities gaining political seats and recognition, or is the Party the political activist for equality and economic freedom? As the pendulum swings to the Democratic Party, social empowerment, economic and individual entitlement constitutes the political interest and policy-making. Many rely on the government as a source of economic sustainment derived in social programs. Have the social programs become hiccups that covertly sequester voters to low socio-economic conditions? Some argue that the Democratic Party, at least, has a platform that contains some benefits in the platform whereas the Republican Party's platform is thought to be dismal and not well defined. Moreover, it is argued that Republican leadership is a result of ideological tokenism. Economic and political gains are intangible and powerless. The beauty of all of this is that you, the informed voter, will decide who is correct.

Most disturbingly, many minorities in the new millennium are unaware of the contributions and the impact on freedom, equality, and justice that many minority pioneers effected on

America. Again, educate yourself and base your political decisions on what you know, instead of what you are being told by those in the decision making arena.

The ability to influence individuals to achieve political and social advancement remains a focal point of political engagement. The unselfish activist action of leaders, during the 1800's and early 1900's, narrowed the political and economic gap. In the fight for inalienable rights, minorities championed the cause of freedom, equality, and constitutional justice for all.

The Road Ahead

What is the future political landscape? The 2014 campaign trail of grassroots politics across one of Georgia's Congressional districts revealed a leadership that seemingly embraced the best candidate irrespective of race. One might surmise that the political fate of a female, running against a male opponent, is subject to historical results. History would indicate that the race would follow historical paths. However, the informed members of the county, state, and national Party indicated commitment to the female candidate who once out the primary would run against an incumbent candidate. The female did not emerge in victory in the Primary election. According to many Party leaders, she was clearly the best qualified candidate. Being the clearly best qualified candidate, obviously, is not a factor for political success. Politics have become grounded in ideo-

logical hatred and political interest. Allegiance to party identity, ill-informed voters, and blindly following rhetoric usurp
the good for all. The female candidate became a casualty in
the political system. She operated in a pseudo political environment; a renowned leader amongst the leaders in her Party. Is tokenism a measure of numbers to base opinion? Are
we clouding the issues of economic, political, and equality
struggles with numbers? The epistemology of Tokenism
must become less to do with numbers and much to do with
self-respect and fighting for political and economic prosper-
ity. We must become unified on issues of substance and not
social belonging. The female candidate ran a campaign on
substance; Educational power, Military power, Political power, economics independence, and social shaping were the
key platform elements.

Education is a vital factor in all facets of life: economical-
ly, socially, and politically. Relationships exist between the
pursuit of educational and professional excellence as a
means of advancement within the society. The income gap
is widening with no political educational solutions. Education
is a factor of economic disparity. The yearly salary of a high
school graduate is $9,300 higher than a high school dropout.
The dropout phenomenon is a factor in the extremely bleak,
economic, and social prospects for many. When compared
to high school graduates, dropouts are less likely to find a
job and earn a decent living wage. The economic and social
dropout-induced conditions lead to poverty, crime, and ad-
verse health conditions. Individual empowerment through

educational self-improvement is a platform issue to break economic, social, and cultural paradigms.

Political power is a major platform issue that can generate a bright future for many in America. The Constitution is the empowering document that establishes the authority of the Federal government to protect citizens' rights, economic framework, and racial justice. Those, depending on the Federal government as the guarantor and enforcer of the principles of inalienable rights, remain resigned to the interest-based decision making of elected representatives. Political power is the driving force behind political, economic, and social liberation. Political power was the cause and is the cause for many that struggle. Political power is a legitimate authority and influence to determine the economic, social, and religious structure and behavior in society. Politicians legislate the making of a nation's educational environment, economic mobility, legal boundaries, and individual and religious freedoms. Politics is a silent means to control education, employment, social conditions, and justice. Political policy lines drawn between *No Child Left Behind* and educational choice drive educational solutions based on improving the American educational system. The internal solutions of teacher evaluations, school assessments, and standardized testing have become the focus of *No Child Left Behind*. However, children fall further behind without incorporating external factors into closing the quality education gap. External, economic, social, and political factors affect educational achievement. Political power and policy accounts for public safety policies, promotes safety and security in the community, and ends bias legal justice systems.

Economic power remains a critical determinate in the future of many Americans. Economic power, void of legitimate coercion, is not an essential differentiator of freedom. Individually derived, economic power reflects the ability to amass wealth irrespective of political and social conditions. Economic power strategies, engrained in political power, is an effective means to bring about meaningful change. A campaign of economic freedom that creates long-term opportunities to eliminate poverty outweighs short-term federal government assistance.

Social shaping is a culmination of Educational power, Political power, and economics independence that determines life experiences and the quality of life. One of the most profound biblical moments in the Bible, other than the Resurrection, occurred in Joshua 5:12. The children of Israel wandered 40 years in the wilderness. During the journey, God feed them with manna to sustain them. Manna fell from heaven each day with the stipulation that the people could only gather what they could eat in a day. However, some missed the significance of this life experience. In Joshua 5:12, God took the manna from the children of Israel; "And the manna ceased on the morrow after they had eaten of the old corn of the land; neither had the children of Israel manna anymore; but they did eat of the fruit of the land of Canaan that year. Some people missed the significance and mistook God's grace for mere providing. During the 40 years of wandering, God purposed His action based on faith and grace and not solely on reliance. *Faith* and *Grace* are empowerment for people to stand on internal substance and not depend on external substance. Politics, in some communities, has to become more than a dependence on government manna. It's time to step into the promise land.

Splintered no more!

Chapter Ten

▰Let's think about
America for a moment!

by: Mack Curry III (Trey)

As you read this chapter, please allow your thoughts to only think about America; not the Political Party you represent.

I leave you to your thoughts my dear associates reading this chapter, I have a comment to make and It concerns the integrity of the Party system. I have always questioned the Party system through and through, simply because it has diminished the strength of the nation's unity and caused more turmoil and blood-shed than any of the great wars of this Earth's history. The Civil War is only one example of how differences in opinions has caused thousands their lives, so why do we allow more aspects to constantly tear us apart. Why do we allow IDEALS, not even physical differences, just a common train of thought to cause us to isolate ourselves from the "non-believers" and take up stands so cemented into the ground that when the opposition has even a remotely "good" idea it is shot down like it had called your mother a liar.

For example, the Affordable Health Care Act, *everyone can agree*, has some problems that need to be worked out. It was said, on National television, that there were some problems; however, just because you happen to be of a different Party, does not mean you have to slander the attempt. Everyone being able to have Health Insurance is a beautiful thing that everyone should love because it will create an equal opportunity for people to enjoy a right to security in their health care. I am not saying you have to put money in people's pockets, but we should not be trying to nickel and dime them for everything they have just so they can have the ability to go to the doctor when they are in dire need of one, and then when they go, be charged for a new house just to get some insulin, or a new catheter, or a new pump, a heart transplant, a pacemaker, you name it. If the insurance does not cover the procedure, people will just opt out of something they truly need simply because they cannot afford it. Insurance companies across the world, guess what, it costs less for someone to go see a doctor once and receive everything they need, than to go to the doctor four times a year, nearly dying at every visit; simply because you would not cover their medical expenses.

So, those of you in politics, stop chanting how you will end what is on the books and start thinking about how to revise, fix, and just make it work without any complications. Make it work to ensure the needs of the people are met, rather than ensuring the sanctity of one's Party reputation. We must stop *"striving to make the government do everything it can for the people".* Stop, please, I am an American too, and I do not need the government doing everything it can for me; I just need it to get out my way as I strive to my pursuit of happiness, and when I fall, should I fall, it is there to catch me, pat me on the back, and tell me what I did wrong and how I can do it different the next time, so I will not fall again. That would be grand, and if any Party can train the government to do that, well, I will support it with full gusto.

Some push people to make their own way and strive for their own happiness. Well, that is awesome for the people who have already done it; but what about that poor teenager on the street who cannot find a job because minimum wage was raised to ten dollars an hour and no business will hire him; no one wants to pay some 17 year old that much money to flip a burger. Chances are, they might not have wanted to drop out of college, but school is expensive and without money it is impossible to go to college; they just have to drop out and then what. If their parents don't let them come back home, then that's it; you have just helped keep a census worker's job because they get to add that teenager to the statistic.

Consider forming a place for people, like that teenager, to go to get the work and money they need, to gain the education they seek, or experience they need, to get a job and make a way for themselves. Trust me, they cannot do it alone with how times are progressing, and if their family is not willing, and there are families that are not willing; then, that is when the Government needs to step in and say, "Hey, I got your back, you will be alright, just dust yourself off, I will help you get to where you need to go. I can show you the door but you must decide whether to walk through it or not".

Enough of what each individual Party should do, let me finish by saying what each Party should have done. I think the best inclination towards what I am about to say is out there, but no one has it all figured out quite yet; so let me say this. "To everyone, no matter your party affiliation, who you are or are not, listen closely. Stop trying to get everything! Stop trying to get the presidency, or control over both Houses, the Courts, the Governor's position, just stop trying to get it all. Instead, just get ENOUGH. Get enough so that when you need to make a policy change, it can be done and not shut down the entire government because people are stubborn and unwilling to compromise. Our entire nation's history is based off Compromises and Treaties and now we have reached the point where 535 men and women on Capitol Hill cannot compromise on any important and country changing legislation. We do not need every detail of AHCA as it is presently written; but, I truly believe it's too late to have it totally abolished. The damage has already been done anyway. Unless we can absolutely regain those things we lost, we just need enough of it to get people the health care they need and not more than the nation can handle.

I walked into an Office Depot the other day and spoke to a man, who worked there, and who I am ecstatic to call an acquaintance. He is establishing his own clothing line and it looks wonderful. He has dreams to take it to New York and get a job as a graphic designer. I asked him when he was leaving, he said in a few months. I said, "Bet you are ready to get rid of this job, aren't you?" He told me this, he said, "Yeah man the pay is not great, but I like what I do. I cannot make this a living, and truly I thought I was only going to have this as a summer job as a way to keep money in my pockets, but the reason why I stayed much longer than I had intended was because I enjoyed the people I worked with, I enjoyed helping people, and what I do is actually quite enjoyable". This was not his dream people, this was not his life aspiration. He did not receive a big fancy check every week, nor did he design clothes like he intended, but he stayed because what he had was good, and not just a little good, it was good enough. He had enough. He didn't need it all. He didn't need a Lamborghini or a Porsche. He did not need to get 240 thousand a year; he just needed enough to survive, to eat, for gas, to continue what he loved to do, and that was sufficient. That was enough for him, before he left to achieve his dreams. I am not telling people to just settle and not achieve their goals in the fastest way possible, but doggone it stop and take a second to enjoy the scenery. It is not fun sitting at the top of the hill if all you can see is yourself. You have millions, great for you, but you don't have love, you don't have friends, you do not even have someone you can call to talk to like a decent human being, without them fearing for the safety of their job. You are alone, and you achieved your dream; but was it worth missing all the great and beautiful opportunities to enjoy life along the way? Just get enough to get you by, enjoy yourself, and then move on to the next bigger and better thing but do not forget to enjoy yourself there as well. Humans by nature do not need everything in the world, they may be greedy, they may be lustful, they may feel envy, but they do not NEED, by the laws of nature, everything they can get their hands on. They just need enough to survive. Happiness is a virtue, but to be sated is a testimony.

The American people must have forgotten what it meant to fight for everything they needed and to be satisfied for what they had. Perhaps the ideal, of political parties, has clouded this mindset and pushed people to believe that they need everything in order to be happy. If our forefathers got along, just fine, in harder times by fighting for everything they needed and nothing more; then how did the American people become so *broken* from each other, not just in the political world, but even from their neighbors? Why are we willing to fight each other when we are all ultimately fighting for the same nation? Another Civil War is not needed to remind people that "achieving all of your goals means restricting someone else's". I don't need the world, I just need enough to get by.

Chapter Eleven

▚It All Begins at Home

by: Chief Andy Rodriguez (USAF Retired)

Simply put, it all begins at home. As we go through our lives, many of our beliefs and habits are shaped by those of our parents or other relatives. For example, the religion we practice is typically that of our parents and grandparents. The places we shop, foods we eat, manner of dress, even sports teams we follow are usually those of our families. The list goes on. If they believe, buy, eat, or cheer for this or that, then it's good enough for me! For the most part, these will guide us through the rest of our lives.

The jobs or professions that we enter into may very well be similar to those of our parents or other relatives. I entered the US Air Force because my father served. My wife also served in the Air Force. One of our sons served in a military branch because of us. A nephew enlisted in another because his grandfather, uncle, aunt, and cousin served. So you can say it's a "family tradition" to serve. It's what we do.

Usually, our leisure activities will be similar to those of our parents. I like to fish because of my father; so do my sons. Growing up, my family traveled a lot. A vacation here, a day trip there, and so on. Because of that, our family enjoys traveling and visiting different places. I like to cook because my grandmothers and parents liked to cook.

Next, neighborhoods or regions shape us, too. Who we are is later determined by our friends and by where we live. Our friends and neighbors will most likely shop where we shop, eat what we eat, dress as we do, and cheer for the same teams. Additionally, aren't the people we work with our closet friends? After all, we're on the same team. Aren't those the reasons we hang around them, or not? If they are from the same geographical region, or of the same race, ethnicity, background, education level, and so on, all the better. After all, they're just like we are!

As we become socially and politically aware, whatever mom and dad identified with, so will we. If mom and dad were life-long members of a particular political party, then odds are pretty good that we'll be members of the same party.   If the folks support a specific social cause, say providing food and clothing for those less fortunate, then we too may support that cause. I know, I became involved with causes for minorities because of my mother's work.

So then, it stands to reason that when we look for candidates to support, we will seek out those that we can identify with: beliefs, social causes, ethnicity, political party, etc. I'm voting for Joe! Joe stands for what I do and he's a member of my party. So what if he didn't keep his campaign promises.

And so it goes for the rest of our lives; that is, until we break from the norm. Then, friendships and other relation-ships fall apart. Allow me to share a few brief examples from my life to illustrate how things became *splintered* at a per-sonal level when it was discovered that my beliefs differed from those of my family, friends, or colleagues.

When I first decided to support the Republican Party in the mid-eighties, I could not believe the blowback I received from the older members of my extended family. My relatives tried to convince me that the GOP was against our people (Mexican-Americans), only cared about the rich, and was bent on cutting or eliminating benefits that they relied upon.   I told them that the party was about hard work, personal responsibility, and fiscal restraint; however, no amount of evidence I could provide could convince them. To this day, I believe we're not close because of our differing political affiliations.   I'm sure there are countless other families with similar situations where politics has broken the family bonds.

Another example for illustration revolves around the metaphor, "Don't judge a book by its cover." When I became involved in a local GOP organization, I couldn't shake the feeling that I was under the microscope. By that I mean, I felt I was looked at suspiciously because of my outward appearance: long braided hair to my waist, as well as a long, gray beard. Actually, a member in attendance remarked that I was at the wrong political party meeting. He said that this was a GOP meeting and not a Democratic Party event.

I don't know if he was joking, or not, but he was judging the book by its cover. Comments such as his do not bring people with similar beliefs together but only serve to drive them apart. How can we unite for a common cause when feelings like this surround us? We can't...the divide widens even though we have shared goals for America.

Another time, my wife and I had been friends with a single parent whose child went to the same high school as our youngest daughter. We all drove together throughout the state as we followed our children's school sports activities. We always had a great time together cheering on the school's teams. Then one day, it all changed.

As we were all loading up to head out to another sports event, the single parent spotted a bumper sticker on the back of our van. It was for a 2008, GOP candidate. Our friend, at that point, said something to the effect that she couldn't believe we were conservatives. She said that we didn't act like conservatives and that Hispanics are usually Democrats. She just couldn't wrap her head around that! Needless to say, shortly thereafter, she no longer hung out with us.

Lastly, I belong to several social and service organizations in the local area. At a recent meeting with one of the groups, I got into a discussion with several members about the focus and direction of the organization. I was arguing my point with another member and it got to the point where neither of us was willing to accept the position of the other. To me, that's fine. I could understand my associate's position and point of view. I just didn't accept it.

Now, understand this, I enjoy and solicit constructive, lively argument and discussion of points of view. How else can we find out how one another feels and what we each believe? To me, it's healthy and ensures the success and growth of a group or organization. My associate did not see it that way. He ultimately ended his participation by saying that I was unwilling to change my position because I am a Republican! How ludicrous is that? I was unwilling to change because he couldn't convince me that his point of view had merit. To this day, he doesn't speak to me or acknowledge my presence at our group's meetings.

I could go on with further examples, but let me wrap it up here by asking a few questions. Because my political beliefs have changed, does that make me a different person? If I take a different point of view than that of my family, friends, or colleagues, does that mean I do not care for the same things that they do? Because I take a conservative approach to life and its challenges and opportunities, does that mean I do not want the same end result as others? The answer to those questions is the same: No!

If we ever want to move our country ahead, we must be willing to understand one another's position and point of view. Then, more importantly, we must understand and accept that even if we disagree, we still want our country to improve. We have to overcome traditions and ideology to mend the *splintering* of America. And, it all begins at home.

SPLINTERED

Chapter 12

▬Project Logic GA

Southern Moderate African American Issues
by: Ted Sadler

Listed below are excerpts from a collection of blogs
written by, and given permission to post by, Ted Sadler.
Many of the blogs will mention the Congressional race of
Vivian Childs.

To read the blogs in their entirety, visit projectlogicga.com.

*Congressional candidate Vivian Childs should be the
great Black hope for the GOP.*

Georgia Election Summit: Put It On the Table
April 12, 2014 by slyram

Everyone has agendas this election year and there is much to sort out. My agenda is based on the best interest of Georgia and the South but the word trump has always been a cornerstone of this blog.

To me, some factors "trump" other factors and the factors of race, faith, region, country, money, and gender can be prioritized 100 different ways by 100 different people. For example, a local congressional candidate from a different party knows person X's interest better than a candidate from X's party from the other side of the area.

. . . .

If I won the sweepstakes, I would use some of that money to convene a summit on the Black agenda for this election year in middle Georgia. The meeting would include folks from both major political parties and of every racial background. While the "Changing Mindset" outline found as a tab at the top of this blog would be the central theme, some other matters need to be put on the table.

Georgia's 2nd Congressional District race: As quiet as it is kept, many Black Republicans know that the voter suppression efforts from their party is hogwash. These good Americans believe that the conservative agenda is in the best interest of everyone and that silly tricks and shady methods drive reasonable people away from their party.

GOP primary voters have the opportunity to select a candidate, Vivian Childs, who might plant the seeds that change the whole political arena. Let's be honest, the GOP often pushes Black candidates who seem a little bland on the Black hand side. With the trump matter in mind, Vivian Childs, Andrew and Deborah Honeycutt, Karen Bogans in Savannah and Michael Murphy are Black Georgians who are conservative but they lived in the Black world, attend Black churches, and likely have Black gold fish. I personally saw Mrs. Childs in fellowship with her sorority sisters, the ladies of Delta Sigma Theta.

Fraternity and sorority trumps political party in my community and you can best believe that the Childs' campaign will never function in a way that dishonors her bond.

....

Childs vs. Bishop would have a residual benefit of showing how to disagree without being disagreeable.

Rep. Sanford Bishop vs Vivian Childs: *Childs, Please*
January 30, 2014 by slyram

A conservative, named Vivian Childs, is running for the U.S. House seat held by Rep. Sanford D. Bishop and I say great. Her candidacy seems like that ant with the rubber tree plant but sometimes it's about the journey.

The people of Georgia have received over three decades of quality service from SDB and I, for one, wish he would have been selfish and left a few years to bring his golf score down and his personal wealth up... think 2 Timothy 4:7 "I have fought the good fight, I have finished the race, I have kept the faith."

Bishop and the Blue Dogs are important targets to the GOP because without them the Dem Team would be as liberal as the far Right pretends they current are. If their silly be---ds listened to me, they would have pushed for SDB to be Agriculture Secretary to get the seat but they wanted to play hardball.

Mrs. Childs' candidacy seems like the type candidacies that Michael Steele wanted to create to gently approach certain areas...

....

Childs and her family seem like wonderful, successful people and her conservatism is rooted in the Black communities of our past—when you knew who you were and whose you were. In those days, shame still existed and you admired how someone "carried themselves."

Here is the real talk: we need some candidates who spend their time listening to and talking with everyone rather than preaching to the choir; candidates who put a positive spin on the limited role of government and fiscal realities. A Bishop vs. Childs race would have a healthy impact on our state and introduce conservative ideals to a new segment of the population. Some people would discover that they are actually more conservative than liberal and that Bishop was moderate to conservative all along.

I am sure the other candidate in the GOP primary in the 2nd District is a decent fellow but Childs opens doors of possibilities that would normally be closed. Ultimately, giving the people choices and options is so beneficial. The first Black GOP member of Congress from Georgia since reconstruction might very well be someone who was introduced to a different way of governing by VC's running for congress....plant the seed.

The New Political Center: oh yeah
October 15, 2013 by slyram

Esquire Magazine and NBC News have produced a study that states what this blog has known for years. Americans don't neatly fit into two political parties and the new political center outweighs a combination of the far left liberals and far right conservatives.

....

This blog has always supported groups and candidates who are about dialog and solutions rather than those who wanted to divide people for their own personal gains.

Invisible Woman, Not Really~

Treat everybody like it may be their last day... It just might be~
-vlchilds

My journey... A journey that really should not exist in a land that preaches one thing, but obviously does another. Faceless, walking forward but moving backwards, being present in a room, yet have no presence; sitting at the table, but having no voice. To put this in perspective, have you tried singing to an offbeat melody while trying to dance on beat?

How do you think it feels to be irrelevant in a world of relevancy, overlooked in an arena of seers, invisible where blindness does not exist? *Welcome to my world~*

The unbelievable commentary in all of this is that with all of the history of disbelief, I actually believed. I believed my Fifth grade teacher when she said you can make it if you are equipped with knowledge. I believed my parents when they said your only limitation in life is you. I believed Dr. Martin Luther King Jr. when he dreamed of the day when all of God's children..., and I believed in the Word when it said I could do all things through Christ who strengthens me.

What was missing in all of the things I was to believe was that those things relied on others doing what was right, that people who would cross my path were also living by those same standards of belief, and that *man or woman,* when given the opportunity, would seek good over evil.

My, my, my:
We hold these truths to be self-evident, that all men are created equal, that they are endowed by their Creator with certain unalienable rights, that among these are Life, Liberty and the Pursuit of Happiness. - *(from the Declaration of Independence)*

Excuse me, please. Am I the only one in the political arena who has read and believed this statement? Everyone talks a sweet game about their principles. These words, a powerful statement, are principles giving a standard of conduct we all should hope and aim to achieve. But do we? Oh, I get it; because it said *men*, many believe *women* are excluded.

I am not quite sure why I thought things would be different if you simply lived right, were a giver instead of a taker, walked the walk, instead of talked the talk, treated individuals with the respect that you expected from others, and followed the laws of the land to the best of your ability.

It has taken me a few gray hairs to get it, but make no mistake about it, I finally got it. I have come to the conclusion that individuals are of no importance or substance unless they are carrying at least a little bit of baggage. People enjoy hearing a story about how someone has overcome obstacles. Again, I get it. I also have always known that simply being good was not good enough in most arenas. My parents, after all, were realists. They assured me that I had to be better than the norm to achieve and be successful. I taught my children the same philosophy and made them aware that even being the best is not always good enough to get or receive what is, for the most part, rightfully yours. Being the best dancer, does not always get you on the team, just as being the best candidate does not get you elected.

I have taken a long look in the mirror to understand why I can see my own reflection but that same reflection is sooo invisible to others. After taking that look, I came to this con-clusion. I have way too many things weighing against me. I am full-figured, married, a non-drinker, a non-smoker, not promiscuous, a female, over forty, short in stature, and oh, by the way, I have integrity.

Anyone who will tell you that those aforementioned things do not matter is not telling you the truth. It does mat-ter. When you read, "About the Author," later in the book, I will give you a synopsis of my community and political in-volvements. Why, to show that I have earned the right to have an opinion in the political arena and to justify, for some, the political run that I sought. What I will not share, is every little detail of how those involvements have impacted lives; I do what I do because there is a need. I do nothing for the accolades of those around me. Remember, some see me as invisible anyway. An advantage of being invisible is being able to watch as things are being accomplished and noticing that the credit for those accomplishments are usually not be-ing credited to the one who has actually done the work, just saying...

There is vision in a visionary~

I remember asking a General, one night at an Officer's club, a long time ago, what else did my husband need to do to be promoted to his next rank (General)? Why? Because, as I listened as people talked about how great he, my hus-band, was, I simply wanted to know what he was not doing to make it happen, so I asked. The General said to me, "Vivian, Henry is one of the best officers I have ever served with, but he will not (you noticed I said not) make the rank of General." He went on to say that, "there are guys who make the rank and there are guys who are responsible for making that happen for others. Henry's reward will be in knowing that he was responsible for getting guys like me promoted to this rank and beyond." Instead of being hurt or disappointed, I celebrated that night with my favorite drink, an orange juice with a shot of grenadine, olives, an orange slice, and cherries on a cute little umbrella pick. I still respect that General to this day for his honesty. Politics, take notice. Instead of overlooking people as if they were not there, be honest and bring things out in the light where they can be seen. I have wanted to share that conversation for many years; Henry, now you know.

Let me add some humor and give you an example of how I know I am invisible. I was at an event with my husband and we were seated in the middle of a long rectangular table. As the serving of the meal began, the waitresses set plates of food in front of everyone who was seated to the left of us. We just knew we were next, not really. The waitresses started serving on the opposite end of the table and served everyone to our immediate right. We just knew that we were next, not really again. Next came the beverages, everyone to the left of us, then everyone to the right of us. I could not control myself as I chuckled. Henry was not the least bit amused as we watched desserts making their way to the guests. Before I could say, "Don't do it," Mister, Colonel, Pastor, Chairman, whatever hat he was wearing at that moment, had gotten up from the table and was coming back with our food. I tried, as best as I could, to remind him that since we are *one* (according to what we preach), then if I am invisible, then so is he. Henry still cannot find the humor in the situation; I, on the other hand, thought it was hilarious and because at that moment *we* were invisible, no one could see me laughing at the ordeal. Wow, to think that this really happened at a large gathering is sad, but true. I could not make this up, even if I tried.

What is worse is to be in a board meeting and make a statement. Absolute silence, no response, no reaction, overlooked. Then out of the blue, someone in the meeting says exactly what you said and everyone reacts with how great an idea that was. Even better, you are having a one-on-one discussion with an individual and make a statement. The individual you are speaking to repeats what you said as if he or she came up with the idea. Just recently, my response was, "How is that different from what I just said?" We have become a *copycat society;* everything you see or hear has been borrowed or downright stolen from someone else.

So, let me set the record straight, I, Vivian L. Childs, some call me Vicky, am not now, nor have ever been, invisible. For whatever reason others choose, it is a choice you know, to ignore those of us deemed invisible, that is on them. It absolutely has nothing to do with us. Actually, there are times that my lack of presence has protected me from things that were to come; I truly thank you for the heads-up.

One of the highlights of my invisible journey is when a Congresswoman pulled me aside at an event *and actually saw me* after an original poem I had recited and said, "You are more than qualified to be a Congressional candidate. What is keeping you from running? "My response was, "*me*." Once again, the remarkable things I have been blessed to achieve, the numerous lives I have touched, the enormous accolades I have received from those needing a hand-up, just for a day, far outweighs the rejections from those who claim they are with me on my journey, but when the time comes to honor their commitment, I am invisible. I do not know if they consciously are doing these things, but the sting, nonetheless from the disappointment, resonates on the inside. During those times, I say, " thank you, Lord, for giving me so much favor, for giving me love, for giving me peace, and for giving me the will to keep it moving, in spite of my invisibility."

I shared in a meeting, when I spoke on why our Party was not reaching people who looked like me. I said, "I am one of you, and you do not always see me, especially if I am not in a Party setting and you definitely never support any of the efforts that I hold dear." In the room were faces of dis-belief. One woman came to me and said, " that cannot be true, Vivian. We love you and I did not know that is how you feel." I said, " it is not a feeling; it is reality, but it's okay." I left that night wondering if speaking the truth would make a difference. If only for a moment, that this group had to open their eyes and see how someone on the inside really felt, then it was worth putting the reality on the table. *Blind no more.* I am so proud to say, that a few from that meeting have now become engaged in community events that help people who can use a little sunshine in their lives and to that I say, *"to God be the Glory~"*

We simply need to educate and stress the importance of looking on the *inside* and not be led by what is on the *outside*. We should not be so *splintered* that we can identify a person's political affiliation by looking on the outside. It happens all too many times. Assumptions are a dime a dozen and judging by what is on the outside can be tricky and misleading. Lisa Roper and Judy Goddard are women who looked and focused beyond what they saw, the outside of me, which allowed them to take a peep on the inside...of me and for that I say, "thank you."

I can laugh now about the many situations where I have felt that I was invisible, *not really.* But, when it was happening to me, not quite so laughable.

Several years ago, a friend of mine, called to say that a gentleman was going to write an article about us. The writer, for once, did not view me as being invisible, quite the contrary. Here is an excerpt from that article:

"The most beautiful woman in the world is smart, sexy, independent and of a free mind." These are the words written by *Shelley Wynter*, a writer who took the time to write the article <u>Real Sisters</u>, about me and three other women. In

fact, he said, *"Besides their commonality on the adjectives I used, they all have one thing in common; they are Black Republicans."*

--------.

He goes on to say that, "These sisters are REAL Black women because like all true Black women they dance to their own beat. Their principles come before what others think about them and finally, when they ask their daughters what they want to be, a singer or Lt. Governor? The answer is always, "I want to be you. mommy."

Beautiful, smart, and independent. Now last but not least, I am NOT saying that these women are better because they are Republicans. I am saying these women are authentic because they believe in a higher principle; that they are not bound by color or victimized by their color.

To clarify and to notify, "I am not invisible, I am, however, an American who loves the greatest country I know." America, you are not perfect, and neither am I. I will say this, I have had an opportunity to visit and live on the soil of many countries and islands. I have not seen any of those places being flooded by visitors seeking citizenship, like we see, daily, in America.

The following excerpt from a poem that I wrote, was inspired by an anonymous poem I read many years ago. It tells how I feel about America and why I strive to fix the *brokenness* that exists.

I Am An American

I am an American
The Constitution is my source of strength.
It has equipped us with the words necessary to lead and
guide this country.

I am an American.

....

I will not apologize for doing what's right, be put aside
without a fight, be sat down, be tossed around, or be
shut down.

....

America,
you can count on me; because I am, an American.

....

Sorrow can't slow me. Disease can't discourage me,
man can't entice me, and lust for fame does not own me;

because, because,

I am,
an American.

Excerpts from *"I Am An American"*: by Vivian L. Childs

Chapter 14

America First; Chartering a New Course

I pray that you will agree that now is the time to realize that the strength of our nation lies with its people. Right now, before, during, and after election cycles, we have an opportunity to bring about real change that works for the people of the United States of America. With every beat of our hearts, we must put America first.

Let us take advantage of this opportunity together. We can and must eliminate the stereotypes and other destructive patterns that we allow, all too often, in America. We, as Americans, accept too much negativity in our political arena. We allow ourselves to be divided and we fail to fully engage in the governing of ourselves while allowing others to bring distress and destruction into our lives. Those who are focused on advancing their own causes and whom are entrenched in their own blinded, partisan, bickering have not accomplished the real change that we the people desire. I say, " It's time to give them a break by sending them back home and away from decision making duties. We need to send people to Washington whose lives have shown a consistent record of standing with and working for the people. True commitment to the people works at all times, not just during election cycles.

Together, let us stand for unity! **Together**, let us stand for jobs! **Together**, let us stand for education! **Together**, let us stand for farmers! **Together**, let us stand against all forms of injustice! Let us stand up and demand better treatment of the men, women, and families who sacrifice their lives each and every day in the military. Let us stand for America! *America first,* PLEASE!

Now the decision is yours.

Had I been elected, in my run for a Congressional seat, my first order of business would have been the acceptance of the oath which states: I do solemnly swear (or affirm) that I will support and defend the Constitution of the United States against all enemies, foreign and domestic; that I will bear true faith and allegiance to the same; that I take this obligation freely, without any mental reservation or purpose of evasion; and that I will and faithfully discharge the duties of the office on which I am about to enter: So help me God.

Oh my goodness; *so help me God.* That phrase really put things in perspective for me. All I could think about was that I was promising, pledging, to do what was right, according to what was written in the constitution (just as it is written in His Word). *What a challenge; what a commitment; what a responsibility!* It reminded me of these words: Surely, goodness and mercy shall follow me all the days of my life...*Putting America first*.

Chapter 15

▉Eyes Wide Open

Don't blink!

The policies of limited government, which implies **the best government is the one which governs the least**, lower taxes, allowing individuals to keep more of the money they earn, and having a strong national defense are the true foundations of a great nation which protects its citizens and their independence. That statement is what I hold on to, which means that the individuals who run on the ticket that declares that statement to be true, should believe the same thing. It is becoming ever so apparent, that that is not always the case.

I am appreciative of the opportunity to participate in the process. I entered the campaign with my eyes wide open. Yes, Rufus, believe me, I really was listening. I was excited to be of service, excited to possibly make a difference, excited to spend long days and nights in an unchartered territory with my husband, yet, delusional on election night. When I ran for the Congressional seat, I was truly running for the constituents in the district. It did not matter to me who my opponent was, I was running for the position, not running against an individual. At the end of the day, once elected, each representative has an obligation to represent ALL with no regard to anything else. I can assure you that I would have served to better the district for *everyone*.

"A vote for me, is a voice for you. Those are the words I spoke while on the campaign trail, those are the words I believed while on the campaign trail. Many of our gains are because of grassroots efforts, I listened to a supporter who spoke of a young woman, twenty two years old, who had never voted. Her reason was that it does not matter. I say to her, "It does matter, every vote matters, every voice matters." I know many are frustrated with politics. Let us use that frustration to make things better. Not only must you vote, you must get your friends, your neighbors, your relatives, and your colleagues to exercise their right by going to the polls to vote.

Our health care system needs to be improved, no one can argue that, but the way it was rolled out and presented was not the best solution for the problem.

What do I believe?

I believe in a strong national defense which protects its citizens and their independence. I believe that every child deserves a quality education, free from bureaucracy and red tape. Teachers should be allowed to teach based on the students' needs, not arbitrary rules and policies set by those who are not in the classroom or in an educational setting.

With eyes wide open, I am on a journey. This train I am riding on started years ago, with values from my parents who are the greatest gift I have ever been given. They instilled in me, and I believed, that the way to overcome the negatives in life was through persistence, through determination, and through personal responsibility.

Personal, meaning the person I would become or the success I would achieve began and ended with me. The mindset of personal responsibility encouraged me to be my best self, trust God and family, and believe that education is the true ladder to success. I encouraged my children and my students to do the same. I taught them to believe in the constitution, trust in God, and treat education like a job. I encouraged them to reach beyond what they could see. I did not allow my children nor my students to blame others if they lacked and more importantly, I taught them that they should not settle when things are not right.

This country, the United States of America, was built because of our diversity. Our greatness is a result of the contributions from all concerned. When there is unity, there is victory. Together, we can make a difference, a significant difference. We must restore our military to its greatness; we must limit government where it is not needed, and we must create opportunities for jobs. Improving schools, maintaining military facilities, and farming and agriculture is of the foremost significance.

What does that mean? That means that the regulations that stunt growth and opportunity must cease. Agriculture is of vital importance in this state. Farmers must have a seat at the table to get the job done to protect their resources.

We must not raise taxes on an already weakened economy. We must find opportunities for jobs allowing our taxpayers to keep more of the monies that they make.

We must now turn beliefs into action.

As well as reaching in, political parties are reaching out to communities like never before. As a Congressional District Chairman, I saw attitudes that were changed because my mission was team-focused; it was about something other than self-gratification. Not only that, even during my Congressional run, I was told by others that I had given them the courage and the confidence to step forward, stand on principles, and be proud; they were given, in a word, hope.

Again, together, we truly can make a difference, a significant difference. We simply need to turn beliefs into action. I know what it's like to fight for basic rights. I watched as college students participated in sit-ins for a better tomorrow for all of us. That is why I stand on my principles and even though the fight has changed somewhat today, I am fighting for our inalienable rights, our God given rights. Everything we need is already in place. We have a constitution that simply needs to be honored, protected, and above all respected.

SPLINTERED

Chapter 16

▶Stay or Retreat

I cannot tell you how many times I have been asked, "Why in the world are you involved in Republican politics? I have been told, " they don't want you and they definitely do not appreciate you." Cynically as it may sound, I live in America and I have the right to choose or not to choose a political party. Saying that, do not think for one moment that I believe that the Party cares if I stay or retreat. In fact, there are many who wish I would never have been in the Party at all. Ask me if I care, I do not. Why, because I am an American and I have that right to choose.

Why in this day and age would we be willing to allow any Party to hold a monopoly on a political party? I would have hoped that those thoughts and those mindsets only existed during the segregation era; must I remind anyone how many years ago that was. A political party should be defined by principles and ideologies; a political party should not be defined by race, age, sex, or any other differences.

For some strange reason, I thought that integration was the *cure all to fix all* that was wrong in America. Integration, in my mind, was to take *brokenness*, the pieces of America that was broken, and put them all together. Instead, we the people have *splintered* ourselves more than ever in this country. This is not, for sure, putting *America first*. According to the dictionary, integration is the bringing of people of different racial or ethnic groups into unrestricted and equal association, as in society or an organization. In other words, integration should have been the glue that put the ugliness, the division among us, hence the *splintered* back together again. Instead, at least in my community, I believe it *splintered* a group of people that had once found solace in working together, a unified harmony into an *I/we have risen* mentality and to heck with everyone else. I am going to get mine, instead of, let's get ours and we will all prosper. We now have a zillion different organizations, serving the same purpose, because everyone wants his or her name in the spotlight.

In my opinion, integration has not entirely done what it was meant to do; however, it was a huge step in the right direction. We have an opportunity, I believe, and there is no time like the present to get it done, and we can get it done if we put America first.

Actually, the things that had once made us strong are now broken into many pieces. I remember the times when, if one person in the community had sugar, if another flour, and if another had milk and eggs, each person would have what they needed to be able to bake a cake. Why, because we had inherited a we mentality and a bond that was unified.

I would be not be telling the truth if I led you to believe that I am not disappointed or frustrated, sometimes, with the way I have been treated. But you know what, I have friends in the other Parties who have had the same experiences as I in their respective Parties; so, I ask each of you, "why do you stay when it appears that it would be easier and less hurtful to retreat."

When I vote, I vote because the people running have or will take an oath to take care of *ALL* constituents, once they are elected. I vote based on the principles that are defined by that Party's definition. Who I am is defined not by Party affiliation, but by whose I am. My decisions are based on His Word and that is good enough for me.

One of the highlights of my political activism is being a Delegate Surrogate at the 2012 Republican National Convention and delivering the first motion from the floor during the convention - *What an honor, what an experience, and what a moment to remember!* Me, a tireless grassroots worker, called to be in a position to shape history and make America a better place for us all.

The answer to a question:

I get invited to many graduations. As I look out amongst the graduating classes, I often wonder what I would say if they were to ask me to speak, what would they want to hear? So, I asked my grandson, Trey, who graduated from high school this year and who wrote chapters for this book, to assist me in a speech that would be thought provoking and millennial. I asked him to share what words, he thought, would impact a graduating class. Here is that speech:

What a time!

Longer than a year, less than a century, shorter than a millennia, greater than a decade; my, my, what a time it has been! As I look into the crowd, I can see the faces of children I have watched grow, develop, learn, and ma-ture...children I would happily call my own. Today is a day that requires a word more convicting than special, and with more attitude than incredible. No, today is a day that is unprecedented. Now, many of you will think of today as the day you are finally free to go off into the world and achieve your dreams, or perhaps many of you see it as a day that starts another journey through education, but this time its "for real". But can we all truly take a second and comprehend why today is unprecedented. People have graduated before, numerous times before, and people have done this journey multiple times in the past, some people have committed to the journey multiple times just in their own life, but none of these people are you. None of those people graduated with you, grew up with you, have taken your classes, had your friends, your teachers, your family, none of them had everything you had, because not just you, or the person next to you, but everyone graduating here today is beyond the normal, far above the usual, and just on the cusp of perplexing. You all, today, are special not just in your own way, but because there will never be a time like this, on a setting like this, with you all doing what we gathered here today to do. You all have walked a long way from kindergarten to now in order to walk up here and take your ticket to a new world. You all have earned this diploma, this piece of paper, this trophy of wood and leaf, this sign that you were able to take a moment, catch your breath, rest your mind, and gather up the strength to pursue life beyond this unprecedented day.

As I pondered that speech, I prayed that none of the graduates would ever have to face the challenges that I face simply because I refuse to become a puppet on someone's entangled string. I am going to stand, even if I stand alone, I will continue to fight, for everyone, regardless of their color, their nationality, their economic status, or their political affiliation. Even the Lord allows us free will, so why should I stifle someone's ability to choose differently than I. As my mother would say, "I do not have a heaven or a hell to put someone in." When it comes to crucifying someone for what they believe, I am not the one. So, looking at today, with a positive hope for tomorrow, *hmmm*, It appears I will *STAY*. To *RETREAT* is not an option.

Yes, Ashante, it seems I have lost my script.

What Must We Do?

F irst and foremost, without compromising principles, we must find a way to bring the message to the people. Too many are saying, "I am done. It doesn't matter, I will believe it when I see it." Okay then, I get it; but I am not done, and together, we, Americans, can and must finish strong. Believe me, things can be done better. The status quo isn't good enough anymore. Someone must lead! Someone must champion the needs of this country. At some point, we must do what is right, because it is the right thing to do.

If we are not taking the lead, then we are trailing behind.

We must restore our military to its greatness; we must limit government where it is not needed; we must ask for quality in schools; and we must create opportunities for jobs. Improving our schools, maintaining our military, creating jobs, and protecting our farming and agriculture should act-ually be of the foremost significance in most campaigns. What does that mean? We must ensure that the regulations that stunt growth and opportunity cease.

Improving our schools means that this country must lead when it comes to education; It must be a priority. Knowing and respecting the value of an education helps. I know the value of an education. As an educator I worked with some great teachers. I can tell you with certainty that tests aren't the answer. We can test students and test them again, but the results will remain the same if there is not a partnership for learning. This country cannot test its way into the lead. We must support teachers and equip them. Tests do not help students learn. Teachers help students learn. So, what is the answer? Great teachers are the answer! One size fits all never fits all; someone always loses out. I refused to let my children lose out. We must refuse to let any child lose out.

School choice for parents must be exactly that, a choice, not a replacement, for our public school system. Our goal should be to ensure that every school provides a quality education for all of its students. The partnership established between home and school is essential. Parents must have a vested interest in their child's education. Let me say this , *"in real estate, location matters; in life, education matters."*

We must maintain our military. The military isn't a just a passion for me, it's a part of me. I grew up in the military. My father served 28 years in the United States Navy and rose to the rank of Senior Chief. My father taught me about personal responsibility, discipline, and sacrifice. I hold those values dear to my heart. Those values have shaped and guided my life. Those values led me to the campus of the University of Georgia, the campus where I met my husband of 42 years. My husband served 30 years in the United States Air Force, reaching the rank of O-6, Colonel. Those were some of the best years of my life. The military afforded me the opportunity to travel the world, make lifelong friends, and give back to the community. The military provided my family and I opportunities that we never would have had. To allow politics to gut our military is not an option. I say "Enough." We cannot renege on the promises made to our veterans. America should not put our current soldiers in harm's way without a significant reason, and America should not weaken the military for our future well-being. We can do better! The problem is, we have far too many people making decisions about an entity they have no clue about. How many elected officials have ever worn a military uniform?

We must protect farming and agriculture. Why? Agriculture is a way of life for many and the number one industry in Georgia; again, farmers must have a seat at the table to get the job done. For example, a group of Black farmers are in a frightening state of losing their farms in this *COUNTRY*. Who will be their voice. Some will say the situation has been settled. I say, "why not have a *full* investigation to see if that is correct." Is there anyone out there willing to take a stand for righteousness and farmers?

If so, contact the American Agriculturalists Association and *do it now!!!!*

We must find another answer to raising taxes on an already weaken economy. We must find opportunities for jobs, allowing our taxpayers to keep more of the monies that they make. The latest two buzz words are minimum wage. Have we really thought about what we are attempting? First of all, minimum wage implies there are jobs, ask the millions of job seekers where are those jobs. Slowly, but surely, the very people we claim those new higher wages are going to help, will soon be without a paycheck. People on fixed incomes will suffer, because the mandate will trigger higher prices, and those who normally benefit from those entry level jobs (those who are new to the workforce, and students seeking jobs) will be *out of a job.*

When will we understand that our government is not responsible for our healthcare, The medical profession is. The Affordable healthcare act, the way it was rolled out, was not well thought out. It was a rush to disaster. Our health care system needs to be improved, but the method in which this was done is not the solution. I, as well as others, understand we need a healthcare system that is accessible and affordable to everyone. More importantly, we need a healthcare system that is run by healthcare professionals who are licensed and trained to save lives. What we cannot do, is while seemingly helping some, we are systematically hurting others. In other words, we are sacrificing Americans for political gain.

Lastly, the fighting and bickering must cease. It has become the cool thing to do. *It really is not.* Many are saying that the children of this generation are out of control and are disrespectful, at church, at school, and even at home. I ask you, "Who are their *Role Models*? Who are they modeling?" If we are truly living in a copy-cat society, and we are, then what the children of this generation see is what the children of this generation will do.

When grown, adult, men and women (many are them are elected official), display childish, out of control, disrespectful behavior on National television and children are watching, why do we expect them to behave any differently. We should not, and they surely do not. I am reminded of the scripture, "you reap what you sow". Simply put, *bad in* results in *bad out.* In some instances, we have rendered parents powerless in the upbringing of their children.

There are many different challenges that generate hope and profit for organizations. I challenge each of you, and I pray you will challenge others, to discipline yourselves to focus on things that are positive. You can communicate and get your point across without compromising your principles and without demeaning the person with whom you are communicating. If we are successful in this challenge, there is hope for the future and we will be amazed by its results. Maybe, just maybe, we can replace frowns and cloudy days with smiles and sunny days. Try it. It just might be the fix the brokenness in our political arena needs.

One American can make a difference, but many Americans, working together, can and will make notable progress.- VLChilds

Chapter 18

▚Before it's too late~

Politically speaking, why now?

had to search my heart to answer this question; politically speaking, why now?

With each passing day, it becomes ever so apparent that, tomorrow might be too late. Politically speaking, what qualifies me to answer this question? Is it the sweat, and sometimes tears, I have poured into the political arena? *Maybe.* Is it because I watch media shows where everyone who has ever had an opinion about the political arena reigns? *Possibly.* Is it because of my political résumé, my political acquaintances, or the many conventions I have attended over the years? *I think not.*

What I have done is simply watched for years as this country has taken a virtual nose-drive in being a good steward of its people; an uncompromising free-fall to the demise of this great country. I have watched, for years, as people have made a career of perpetuating a drive for self-gratification, instead of what is best for the country as a whole. The story of Humpty Dumpty comes to mind except, unlike Humpty, I and the other contributors to this book are coming down off of the wall with a message for our readers before America falls, and we are not able to put her *splintered* pieces back together again; *all for political gain.*

I never, ever, ever would have imagined that merely because of one moment spent in an election booth, to cast a vote for representation, that it would cause an American to be loved by some and despised by others. A simple vote, mind you, a declaration of a political party, would result in political suicide. Who would ever have imagined? Surely, not I.

It is amazing how many will speak of unity, brotherhood, and/or sisterhood, yet engage in divisive actions that is on a collision course to destruction. We, as Americans, can and should do better,

In every county, in every district, in every state, no matter the size or the amount of people, everyone should have an equal voice at the table and we need to nurture and grow our strengths to continue the goal of recruiting and electing qualified individuals. Electing qualified individuals should be based on character and something other than how much capital can be raised in a given election.

Again, **unity** is the key to success and together we are better inclined to make successful decisions for America.

Politically speaking, it is to be duly noted that I know that the political arena is broken. I also think that you, the reader, know that the political arena is broken. So, what are we doing? Are we going to do nothing to mend the broken madness or are we looking for solutions? Finding solutions would be beneficial because I am fairly sure, that we also realize, that we will indeed sacrifice America for political gain if we do not. *Now what?*

Are we willing to do what is necessary to halt this political upheaval? Can we halt playing Russian roulette with our children's future? Is the brokenness worth fixing, or are we destined to be *splintered*?

The answer lies with you and those around you. Remember, tomorrow might be too late. Are we really willing to sacrifice America for political gain?

About the Author
Vivian L. Childs

I am married and through our union, I birthed three remarkable children and have nine lovely grandchildren.

When I left the wonderful world of teaching, my goal was, and still remains, to motivate and elevate. Today, that is the mission statement of my business, "UICF.' I have been fortunate to watch individuals accomplish their goal of getting a GED through my business' Learning with Love program. Before entering the program, for some students, it was everyone else's fault why they left school except their own. The goal is to teach individuals to go beyond what looks impossible.

I believe that if you set goals, if you do the things necessary to achieve them, and if you live a life according to scripture, your life will prosper.

I believe in the principles of freedom and liberty for all; isn't that why this country was established in the first place?

Through the years, I have prided myself on being a pusher. I have pushed integrity, I have pushed personal responsibility, and most importantly, I have pushed love.

A Synopsis of my Community Involvement

- Arts Alliance: *President, Vice-Pres., Grant Writer*
- Appointed to Houston County Board of Elections
- Technical College Adult Ed Advisory Board
- Youth, Science, Technology Board
- ROAL: *Department of GA State President/Secretary,*
- Military Affiliations: *OWC/OSC President, Parliamentarian, Thrift Shop advisor, Thrift Shop chairman, Protocol Officer, Magazine editor, Air Force Village representative, organized a children's Breakfast with Santa program ; Logistics Group advisor; Singer for various Base events; BX and Commissary Representative; PWOC speaker; Religious Education Coordinator; Base Tax Assistance volunteer; Family services; Red Cross; created, directed and coordinated a" Miss Teen Pageant" for eight years;*
- School District Affiliations: *High School Booster Club President; Parent representative at the (KIDS) Coalition Rally; " I Make The Difference Employee/Volunteer Recognition Awards Selection Committee"; Building Improvement Team; Parent Teacher Organization President; Peer-Counseling Training; Served as the Community Education Liaison with Air Force Base; Enrichment Brochures Coordinator; Developed a quarterly brochure for Community Education; Co-chaired the Community Education Council (met monthly with the Superintendent of Schools to develop agenda); co-developed a Job Assistance Committee; WCA School Board*
- National Military Family Association representative.
- Recognized during Women History/Black History events
- "Key to the City" recipient
- National Anthem singer at community functions

A Synopsis of my Political Involvement

- Chairman of Georgia's Eighth Congressional District:
- Charter President of Middle Georgia Republican Women
- Vice-chair of 2013 NFRW Summer SE Regional Conference, "United We Stand"
- 2013 Bridging the Gap Women's Summit speaker
- Delivered the 1st motion from the floor, as a delegate surrogate, during the 2012 National Republican Convention
- Panelist for the first Georgia Black Conservative Summit
- Parliamentarian for various groups
- Served on the GAGOP State and Executive committees
- Served on Local GOP Executive committee; Precinct chair;
- Represented the Republican's views during a political forum.
- Served on the Protocol and Distinguished Guests Committee of the National Federation of Republican Women
- Georgia Federation of Republican Women: Rules and Bylaws chair, Protocol chair, Parliamentarian
- Grass root organizer and boots on the ground: *campaign headquarters worker, phone banks, mail outs, office volunteer, sign waving, poll watcher, stuffed envelopes, licked stamps, made phone and computer calls, hosted college students (campaign workers) in my home*
- Planned, decorated, and assisted with political events and fundraisers for elected officials
- Women coalition county chair/advisory
- Assisted in planning an organized statewide political event
- Selected for United States Senatorial campaign television commercial
- Featured on multi-state billboards
- A regular guest for radio and television interviews
- National Anthem/Patriotic singer

The Contributing Writers

Many, many thanks to all of the following who I believe, believe as I believe, that unless we unify to make America whole and not a scattered array of ideas, lacking camaraderie, we will continue spiraling downward.

Nicholas Buford, Colonel Henry Childs *(Ret)*, Mack Curry III (Trey), Nakeisha M. Curry M.D., Ashante Y. Everett, Chief Andy Rodriguez *(Ret)*, Ted Sadler

Thanks also to: Alexis Childs, Henry Childs II, Helen Clark, Aralyn Everett, Gordon Everett, & Shelley Wynter.

You are my *Heroes and Sheroes*.

Contributing Writer

Nicholas Buford

Nicholas Buford was born and raised in Cordele, GA. He currently attends Valdosta State University; where he is working to receive a degree in Political Science. In addition to being a full time student, Nicholas serves as the Vice President of the student body at VSU. After graduating from VSU, Buford plans to attend law school. In February 2014, Nicholas Buford was hired as an administrative assistant by Property Tax Eagle, a prominent property tax firm that fights for low-income housing residents across the Southeastern United States. Nicholas has loved politics ever since the eighth grade. He has served in numerous class elective offices and leadership positions. He works in numerous capacities for different political campaigns within the state of Georgia.

Above all, Nicholas Buford is overjoyed to be a child of God. The son of a Baptist pastor, Nicholas has been in church his entire life. More importantly than being in church, Nick has seen lives changed, people healed, and so much more. He's a firm believer that there is not a single person out of the reach of God's grace. Day by day, Nicholas prays to grow closer to Christ, live in a way that is more pleasing to him, and commit to God's master plan. One of his favorite Bible verses is Jeremiah 29:11 " For I know the plans I have for you," declares the Lord, "plans to prosper you and not to harm you, plans to give you hope and a future."

Contributing Writer

Colonel Henry Childs (Ret)

Colonel Henry Childs holds a Bachelor degree in Political Science from the University of Georgia, a Masters Degree in Human Resource Development from Webster University, and is currently in the final stages of pursuing a Doctorate Degree in Business Administration.

He is the Senior Pastor of North Bethlehem Missionary Baptist Church and President of Because We Care II. In addition to spreading the life changing Gospel of Jesus Christ and meeting the needs of the total person (spiritually, physically, and emotionally), he leads a team that inspires educational success for at risk youths. He has served on several boards and has been the speaker for community events across the country.

Colonel Childs has 30 years of military service with more than 2,700 flying hours in the B-52 and B-1B aircrafts. He held a variety of command executive positions. He was responsible for organizing, training, equipping, and providing for the welfare of more than 59,000 Airmen in maintenance, supply, transportation, contracting, and logistics plans career field. As Commander of the Defense Information System Agency, Western Hemisphere Logistics Support Center, he led the DoD in operational excellence by consolidating 42 information processing centers into 16. His efforts saved the DoD $474M in operating costs and $61M in recapitalization equipment. As a Logistics Group Commander and Senior Analyst, he was responsible for incorporating Lean Six Sigma methodology in Logistics operations that include aircraft depot maintenance and supply chain management. He holds a *Lean Six Sigma Black Belt Certificate.* Colonel Childs was responsible for logistics business reengineering: Led USAF logistics re-organization, established first-ever U.S. Air Force Reserve Logistics Readiness Center to meet wartime resource deployment, led and re-engineered aircraft maintenance phase process, and led human resource right sizing and training for Air Force logistics personnel.

After retiring in 2004, Colonel Childs became a Government contractor. He was recognized as a lean logistics "expert" where he won Contractor of the year.

He and his wife, Vivian, of East Point, GA, have three children: Nakeisha, Ashante, and a son Henry II. Son Demetrius passed away in 2008. They have nine grand-children.

Contributing Writer
Mack W. Curry, III

Mack W. Curry, III (a.k.a "Trey") graduated from Foothill High School in Henderson, NV with an Advanced Honors Diploma in 2014. He is an esteemed percussionist who led an internationally ranked drumline during his high school career. He has performed alongside legends such as Gloria Esteban and Trace Adkins. After high school, he was awarded a Congressional internship and he also served as an intern for a Victory office in Georgia. Trey will be attending the University of Georgia in January. His ultimate final educational goal is to earn a Juris Doctorate.

Contributing Writer
Nakeisha M. Curry, M.D.

Dr. Nakeisha Curry is a dual-trained physician in the fields of Internal Medicine and Pediatrics. She graduated from residency at the University of Kansas in 2005 and currently practices medicine as a Hospitalist in Las Vegas, Nevada.

Dr. Curry has received numerous awards highlighting her outstanding service and quality medical care. She has also been recognized as one of the "Leading Physicians of the World".

Dr. Curry attributes her success to her faith in God and uses the following philosophy to guide her therapy: Health comes from within. Therefore, if you heal the mind and spirit, the body will follow

Dr. Curry is the proud mother of two dynamic children and she is a minister.

Contributing Writer
Ashante Y. Everett

Ashante Everett was born on the island of Guam. During her senior year of college, she was selected to be the lead teacher in an after-school dance program. Because of the opportunity she was given to make a difference in the lives of so many young students, she embarked on a career in teaching.

Ashante's heightened interest in dance began early in her childhood and came full circle after receiving her Bachelors of Arts degree, in dance, from the University of Kansas. She then traveled to Terceira (a Portuguese island) to study under the Island's renowned Ballet instructor

Eduardo Rosa. After training in Portugal, Ashante decided to take a year off to tap into her second love, writing.

Who would have ever thought, that after taking a year off to write a book, Ashante would be hired as a dance teacher at Westport Edison Middle School in Kansas City, Missouri? To her surprise, it turned out to be an elective class (like art or music) at a traditional public middle school, not a technical dance class at a fine arts school like she had thought. Westport gave her the inside look at a career in teaching that is complex, challenging, yet very rewarding. Due to the rewards outweighing the challenges, Ashante refocused, exited the world of dance, and began a career in teaching.

Ashante showed dedication and drive in teaching which led to a Master's degree in Education and an Educational Specialist degree in Educational Leadership. In addition to her collegiate studies, Ashante stays abreast of trends and policies in the field of education by extending herself to several organizations centered on education.

Ashante has been recognized, by many, for her skills and knowledge as it relates to curriculum, instruction, and professional learning. She received an Outstanding Women in Education Award, in 2012, and was presented this honor by the event's special guest, Georgia's First Lady, Mrs. Sandra Deal.

Contributing Writer
Chief Andy Rodriguez

Andy Rodriguez was born at Fort Worth, Texas. During his early years he lived in Japan, Spain and Panama. After graduating from Balboa High School, Canal Zone, he enlisted in the United States Air Force and served for 32 years retiring as a Chief Master Sergeant. Assignments found him all over the globe, to include flying combat and combat support missions over Afghanistan, Bosnia-Herzegovina, Croatia, Kuwait and Saudi Arabia.

Andy has a Bachelor's degree, majoring in Political Science, from the University of Nebraska at Omaha and a Master's degree in Human Resource Management from Troy University. He and his wife and family reside in Warner Robins, Georgia.

Contributing Writer

Ted Sadler

Ted   Sadler is a native of Sylvester, Georgia, and holds an AA from Darton College and BA and MPA from Albany State University.

Ted worked in the United States Congress in Washington DC in the offices of Rep. Charles Hatcher, Rep. Don Johnson, and Rep. Sanford Bishop. He later returned to Albany State to serve as Program Director in a community development center. His blog **Projectlogicga.com** emphasizes southerners bridging the political, cultural, and social divide.

My grandmother, Vivian Childs, is a wonderful, intelligent, and determined woman. She is a great person to talk to and is a great listener. She is very motivated and motivates others. She is a down to earth type of woman and is just a great person altogether.

Love You, Grandma,
Alexis Childs
Author of Sky Phoenix

Acknowledgements

Many, many thanks to everyone whom I am blessed to have in my life, especially the Lord and my family. A huge thank you to those who attended my campaign announcement, to those who sent donations, to those who made countless phone calls, to those who placed signs in your yards or at your place of business, to those who hosted or attended fund-raising events, to those who endorsed me, and to those who prayed.

A special thank you to Henry Childs and Judy Dienst. These two individuals travelled the district, at their own expense, as surrogates for my campaign. They spoke, in my absence, on numerous occasions.

Judy Goddard, I would never have gotten so involved in the Party without your mentorship and your arms wide-open friendship.

Vivien Scott, Sue Everhart, Kaye Goolsby, Linda Herren, Lisa Roper, Gloria Alday, Linda Shingler, Missy Shorey, Angela Hicks, John House, Tom Morrill, & Earle Shivers, thank you for your wisdom.

Soul Sisters: Elaine Pritchard, Lisa Roper, Lelia Hagood, Pamela Bohannon, Yvonne Foreman.

Campaign team: Tonya Boga, Michael Murphy, Prisca Villa, Taylor Johnson, Mandy Chaney, Camilla Moore, Campaign & County Chairs .

Across the miles: Sandra Zimmerman, Margaret Jones, Angie Pinder, & Kheron Jones-Kassing, a successful godchild who has never needed anything from me; I have simply always prayed for her and God has indeed shown her favor.

Thank you Renee Elmers and Palladian View's *Bridging the Gap Women's Summit.* Speaking at the event sparked my campaign journey~

Matthew Denson of Print2Draw and the talented Jamie Jordan for assisting with graphics when needed

Laurie Bremner, Linda Clements, Ester Denson, Lanitra Menefee, Fenika Miller, Maggie Newberry, Ruby Robinson, Donna Sant, Eddie Slaughter, Linda Umberger, Sharon White, Rose Wing, the Morrison-Carlton Family & (AB, AR, BL, EC, DH, JH ,KC, LS. MM, RA, RT, SH) for believing.

My friend, the beloved Rick Richardson, you will be remembered~

Please feel free to contact us if you would like information on any of our products and services. If you are interested in having one of our writers, or the author speak at an event, please visit our website **(www.vivianlchilds.com)** and submit a speaker's request form.

You may also request by mail/email:

VLCHILDS/UICF, LLC
PO Box 9334
Warner Robins, GA 31095

email: splintered@vlchilds.com

Phone: (478) 953-9767

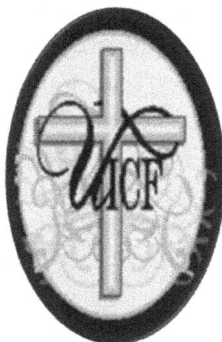

Sky Phoenix

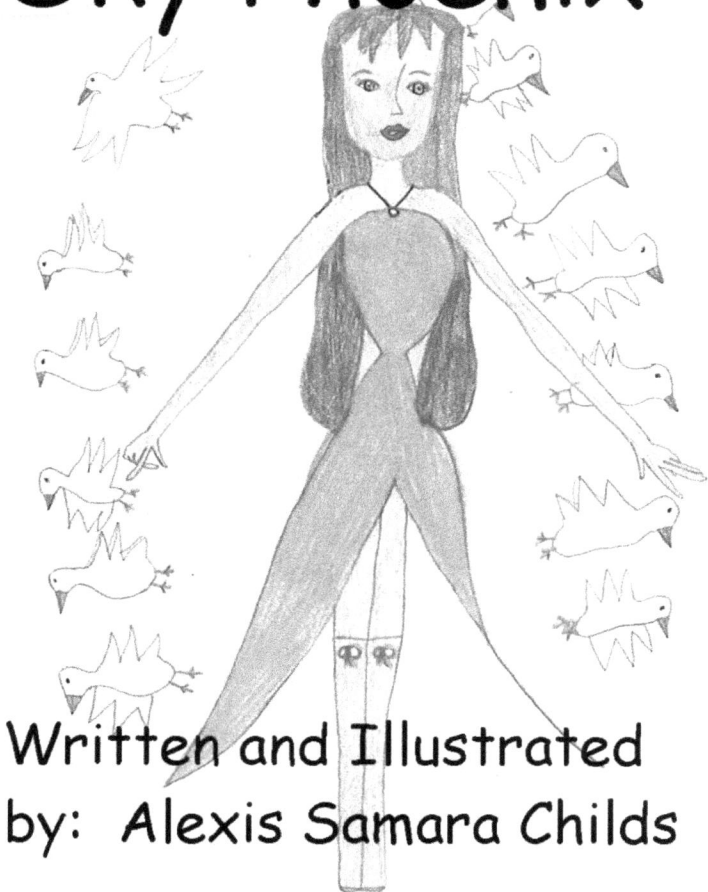

Written and Illustrated
by: Alexis Samara Childs

You may purchase this book for $9.95. Great reviews
from children, parents, and grandparents.

The Grand Bombaray

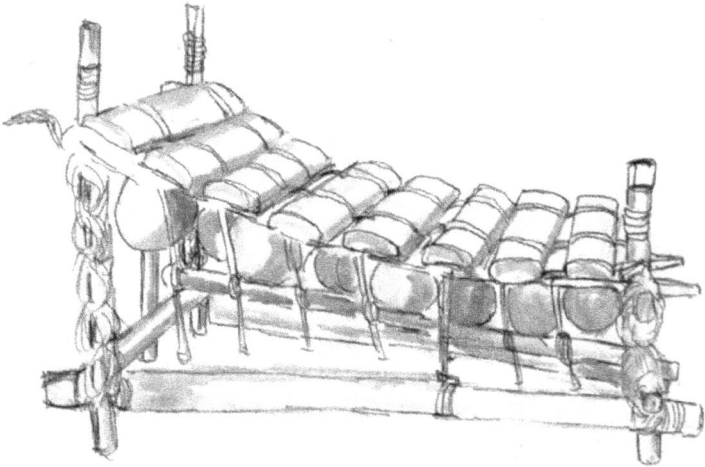

By: Nakeisha M. Curry, M.D

Illustrated by: Peggy Vesely

You may purchase this book for $12.95. Great reviews!

TITLE: THE GRAND BOMBARAY

AUTHOR: NAKEISHA M. CURRY, M.D.

PRICE: $ 12.95

PUBLICATION DATE:9/14/2008

ABOUT THIS BOOK:

STIMULATE YOUR MIND WHILE CHILDREN PLAY. FIND SITARS,CARNIVAL TREATS, AND SHEKERES. JOURNEY THROUGH PERRY WHERE MYCHILDREN STAY AND TRAVEL TOGETHER WITH THEIR GRAND BOMBARAY!

I AM AN AMERICAN
by Vivian L. Childs

I am an American

The Constitution is my source of strength.
It has equipped us with the words necessary to
lead and guide this country.

I am an American.

....

I will not apologize for doing what's right,
be put aside without a fight, be sat down,
be tossed around, or be shut down.

....

America,
you can count on me;
because I am, an American.

....

Sorrow can't slow me.
Disease can't discourage me,
man can't entice me,
and lust for fame does not own me;

because,   because,

I am,
an American.

Signed copy its entirety. $5.00

SPLINTERED

www.ingramcontent.com/pod-product-compliance
Lightning Source LLC
Chambersburg PA
CBHW072012290326
41934CB00007BA/1063